THE

cast iron skillet

COOKBOOK

Updated & Expanded Edition

— The —

Cast Iron Skillet

COOKBOOK

Updated & Expanded Edition

RECIPES *for the* BEST PAN
in Your Kitchen

**SHARON KRAMIS &
JULIE KRAMIS HEARNE**

Photographs by Charity Burggraaf

SASQUATCH BOOKS
SEATTLE

for elsie—mother, grandmother, and great-grandmother—who inspired us to continue cooking in the cast iron skillet —s. k. and j. k. h.

Printed in China

Published by Sasquatch Books
17 16 15 14 13   9 8 7 6 5 4 3 2 1

Editor: Gary Luke
Project editors: Nancy W. Cortelyou
and Rachelle Longé McGhee
Photographs: Charity Burggraaf
Design: Anna Goldstein

Library of Congress Cataloging-in-Publication Data is available.

ISBN: 978-1-57061-905-2

Sasquatch Books
1904 Third Avenue, Suite 710
Seattle, WA 98101
(206) 467-4300
www.sasquatchbooks.com
custserv@sasquatchbooks.com

CONTENTS

ACKNOWLEDGMENTS

TO MY DARLING DAUGHTER JULIE, who loves to cook. We have so much fun sharing food experiences together. To my husband, Larry, who was our taster and food critic. To my sons, Joe and Tom, and their families, who appreciate gathering together to cook and share good food. A very special thanks to Marion Cunningham, who invited everyone to the table for a memorable meal. To all of our friends at Anthony's Restaurants, with respect and appreciation for their commitment to quality and community. —*S. K.*

TO MY COAUTHOR, MOM, AND FRIEND, who took me through the looking glass into the wonderful world of food. A special thanks to my supportive husband, Harker, and my little taste testers, Reilly, Konrad, and Andrew. —*J. K. H.*

a note to our readers

IN OUR FAMILY, we are part of three generations of women who have been cooking side by side for many years. We love to cook. We can always be found shopping for food, cooking food, talking about food, or reading food magazines. Our favorite outing is a visit to our local farmers' market. We load up our baskets and plan our menu for that night's dinner. It's our passion, and we discover something new each time we cook, usually in the cast iron skillet. We hope you will rescue your cast iron skillet from the garage or back cupboard and enjoy the sounds and smells of cooking the recipes in this book.

INTRODUCTION

It's a wonderful thing to step into a friend's kitchen and see a cast iron skillet on the stove. You know right then that you are going to have something delicious to eat, that you are in the home of a true cook. A cast iron skillet has an heirloom quality about it. Every pan has its own stories to tell, memories of sharing great meals with friends and loved ones. No other pan has this kind of history. Passed from generation to generation, old cast iron skillets remind our senses of smells and flavors that make us want to heat them up and hear them sizzle with good food again.

The cast iron skillet is one of the most important pans in your kitchen. It is the key to good cooking. We'll admit up front that a cast iron skillet is heavy and a bit more difficult to clean and maintain than a skillet coated with Teflon or other nonstick material. So why use it? For browning, searing, roasting, and caramelizing, we have greater success with cast iron than with any other kind of pan. Certain recipes require an iron skillet; others just taste better when cooked in one. Cast iron's unique characteristic of producing dry, even heat makes it ideal for baking as well. Baked goods come out moist on the inside with a crisp, golden crust on the outside. Vegetables roast and caramelize perfectly. Meats sear and brown just as they should and don't seize up or stew because cast iron doesn't cause additional moisture to form.

For three generations the cast iron skillet has played an important role in our family. Sunday mornings always meant peeking into the oven to watch the Dutch baby rise, the sautéed apples and powdered sugar waiting on the table. We've included many of our favorite recipes that have been in our family for years. Our well-seasoned cast iron skillets connect our family history with love, one generation to the next.

Here we present to you our classic family favorites alongside adventurous new dishes with ingredients that bring together flavors from around the world. You will find recipes that are timeless and versatile, and cooking them in cast iron makes all the difference.

The cast iron skillet is the reason cooks are making tarte tatin in France, tortilla Española in Spain, rösti in Switzerland, and Irish soda bread in Ireland. These old-world dishes were made in cast iron more than a hundred years ago, and cooks are still making them in cast iron today, with good reason.

It's time to rediscover the cast iron skillet. Whether yours once belonged to your grandmother or is a new preseasoned pan fresh out of the box, use it and enjoy it; it will only get better with time. Best of all, you'll find that it will bring generations together to cook, share good food, and create lasting memories.

YOUR CAST IRON PAN

CAST IRON COOKWARE HAS BEEN AROUND FOR HUNDREDS OF YEARS. Centuries ago, cast iron kettles and skillets were used over open fires in Europe. They were some of the very few treasured items that settlers brought with them to the New World.

Cast iron pans are formed through the process of sand casting. Molten iron is poured into a sand-clay mold of the desired shape. After it cools, the mold is removed and the pan's surface is smoothed by a stone-washing process. Pioneer cast iron companies Griswold, Wagner, and Lodge Manufacturing were the leaders in cast iron cookware. Today, Lodge, founded in 1896, is the largest domestic producer of high-quality iron cookware. Lodge products are readily available in cookware shops and hardware stores throughout the country. You can occasionally discover them at secondhand stores.

Cast iron pans come in a wide variety of shapes and sizes to suit almost any culinary need. We recommend pans from Lodge that are made in the United States. Their pieces range from skillets, Dutch ovens, grill pans, and griddles to specialty pans for breads, casseroles, and muffins. French-made Le Creuset's enamel-coated cast iron cookware, which is more expensive than traditional cast iron, is our favorite for soups and casseroles. Staub cast iron, also made in France, produces unique cast iron pieces sold in many different shapes and sizes. Both Le Creuset and Staub are available at specialty cookware stores such as Sur La Table (see Resources, page 189).

Often, cooks who are unfamiliar with cast iron are pleasantly surprised to find that well-seasoned cast iron has a perfect nonstick surface. Teflon-coated and stainless steel pans tend to cause food to "sweat," which stews and toughens meat instead of browning it, and prevents a crisp crust from forming. Food cooked in cast iron doesn't sweat. Cast iron pans heat quickly and evenly and maintain their heat. They provide an even exchange of heat with the food, thus allowing meats to brown and caramelize. The high heat of the pan forms golden crusts on baked goods and acts just like a wood-fired oven for pizzas and breads.

Cast iron's versatility is what appeals to us the most. We use our cast iron skillets for pan-searing, pan-roasting, stir-frying, and baking. We find that an iron skillet is an excellent alternative to a wok—especially for those who cook on an electric stove. For camping, cast iron pans are indispensable. A Dutch oven is perfect for cooking over an outdoor fire, and it can be used either as an oven or as a slow cooker.

purchasing cast iron cookware

TODAY, MOST NEW PANS COME PRESEASONED, which means you can use them right out of the box. Even a preseasoned pan, however, will need to be reseasoned now and then to maintain its nonstick surface. Unseasoned new pans are gunmetal gray in color, but with proper care and much use they will develop the familiar black patina that is the hallmark of a well-seasoned skillet.

You have a lot of choices when shopping for a new cast iron pan. Keep in mind that you don't need every shape and size. We own 8-, 10-, and 12-inch skillets—two with straight 2-inch sides for searing and roasting, and one with 4-inch sides for stewing and braising. We love our griddle pan for pancakes, bacon, and eggs cooked side by side. A grill pan is our indoor barbecue, perfect for grilling meats of all kinds.

Here are descriptions of our favorite skillets and pans. Note that most cast iron skillets do not come with lids. When we are in need of a lid, we use one from our cupboards that is the same size as the pan.

SKILLETS are generally straight-sided and long-handled, with sizes ranging from 6½ inches in diameter and 1¼ inches deep to 15¼ inches in diameter and 2¼ inches deep. (Sizes are indicated on the bottom of the skillet.) Large skillets have loop handles on either side, which make them easier to manage.

Lodge also has a stir-fry skillet, which resembles a wok and is 12¾ inches in diameter and 3¼ inches deep. If you like wok cookery, you'll find that this cast iron version works well on both electric and gas ranges.

GRILL PANS, both round and square, have raised ridges in the bottom of the pan, which make them ideal for cooking boneless, skinless chicken breasts, fish fillets, and flank steaks indoors. These pans are a wonderful alternative to an outdoor grill. Sizes range from 9 inches in diameter to roughly 11 inches in diameter; they are approximately 2 inches deep.

DUTCH OVENS have loop handles and always come with lids. They are approximately 4 to 5 inches deep and range in capacity from 5 quarts to 9 quarts. Note that Dutch ovens differ from "camp ovens" or "spiders." Camp ovens are deep like Dutch ovens but have three legs for setting on an open fire. (Dutch ovens have flat bottoms.) We have become reacquainted with our Dutch oven, and we use it indoors as well as outdoors. Lodge makes a great preseasoned, 6-quart Dutch oven perfect for stews and soups.

GRIDDLES are flat with smooth surfaces. Some have grill ridges on one side. Our favorite is rectangular in shape and fits over two burners.

You will also find specialty cast iron pans used for specific recipes. The specialty pans we own are a popover pan, an ebelskiver pan, and a Swedish pancake pan. Season specialty cookware as you would any other cast iron pan, and always use a little butter or vegetable oil before adding batters.

caring for cast iron

NEVER WASH A SKILLET IN A DISHWASHER! Sometimes, especially after cooking egg dishes, you will have to briefly soak the skillet before scrubbing. Never use metal to scrape the pan.

To clean and care for your cast iron skillet after each use:

1. Hold the pan under hot water, and scrub it clean with a nylon scouring pad or a stiff-bristled plastic brush. If you've cooked fish in the skillet, add a few drops of liquid soap and rinse well with hot water.

2. Dry the pan immediately with a towel or on the stove top over medium-low heat, and rub it lightly with olive oil to keep it from drying out.

3. Line the pan with a paper towel, and store it in a warm, dry place. Store lids separately to allow air to circulate around the pan and lid to prevent condensation,

which can lead to rust spots, or keep your pan in the oven; every time you turn it on, the pan will reseason itself.

4. If food begins to stick, soak the pan briefly in warm water and scrub it clean with a stiff-bristled plastic brush.

If you find a rusted cast iron pan at an antique shop or garage sale, you *can* rescue it. Simply scour the pan with a nylon scouring pad or stiff-bristled plastic brush, and then rinse under hot running water. Dry thoroughly with a towel. Rub the pan with olive oil, using a paper towel to distribute it evenly; repeat several times until a paper towel comes out clean. To remove residue buildup, put the pan in a large pot of boiling water with 1 cup baking soda and boil for 10 minutes, then scrub with a nylon scouring pad and reseason your pan.

reseasoning cast iron cookware

THE SECRET TO SUCCESSFUL COOKING in cast iron is proper seasoning and care for your pans. The point of seasoning is to bake the fat into the pan's porous surface to create a smooth, permanent nonstick coating and to prevent rust.

Follow these steps for reseasoning an old pan:

1. Dry the pan thoroughly, and coat it lightly with Crisco shortening, inside and out. (We don't recommend using vegetable or other liquid oils, as they can leave the pan sticky.)

2. Place the pan upside down on a baking sheet on a rack in the middle of the oven. Bake for one hour at 350°F. The pan will smoke, but the smoke will disappear after 20 minutes. Be sure to have your oven fan on. You can also do this on a baking sheet on your barbecue, with the lid closed.

3. Turn off the heat, and let the pan cool completely in the oven.

The first few times you use a newly reseasoned pan, it's best to fry bacon or other fatty foods. After these first uses, you'll find that your pan will develop a permanent nonstick surface.

cooking with cast iron

CAST IRON HEATS VERY EVENLY, so you don't need to cook at high temperatures. Most of the time we use medium heat.

Remember that the handles of cast iron pans get hot, so keep oven mitts close by when using a skillet. Because the pans are heavy, always use two hands (and two oven mitts!) when lifting a hot skillet. Cast iron stays hot long after it has been removed from the heat, so remember to use a trivet when placing your pan on a table or countertop.

When you are ready to cook, heat your cast iron skillet or mold pans over medium heat before adding oil or food to the pan. To test the heat, sprinkle in a few drops of water: the droplets will dance across the pan.

When cooking dishes with marinades, sauces, or glazes in cast iron, be sure to rinse the pan with hot water immediately to prevent residue buildup. If the inevitable buildup occurs, you can scrape the pan with a plastic spatula to remove any black bits. Then rinse the pan, dry it well, rub with oil, and store.

Don't store food in a cast iron skillet because the pan will impart a metallic taste. Always remove food and wash the pan immediately after cooking.

Cast iron pans do demand a bit of care, but once you've cooked in one, we're certain you will agree that they are well worth the effort.

BREAKFAST
& BRUNCH

If you have fond memories connected to a cast iron skillet, they probably have something to do with breakfast. The smells of sausage and eggs cooking in a cast iron skillet are a wonderful greeting in the morning.

We can't say it enough: so many foods are at their best when cooked in cast iron. Because cast iron conducts heat so evenly, bacon gets crisp and pancakes come out golden brown. Coffee cakes are golden on the outside, incredibly moist on the inside.

Take a few minutes on Saturday afternoon to prepare Overnight French Toast. Sunday morning, your family can enjoy making breakfast together. Other recipes can easily be made during your first cup of coffee. Our family likes to use the big cast iron griddle to cook pancakes and sausages side by side.

So make some coffee, pour the fresh-squeezed orange juice, heat up your griddle, and enjoy a leisurely breakfast with your family.

classic buttermilk pancakes

Saturday morning is pancake time. Weekdays are so busy; it's fun to relax and enjoy a leisurely breakfast when the weekend rolls around. The cast iron skillet or griddle cooks perfect pancakes every time. Sprinkle fresh blueberries or huckleberries on top of the pancakes while they are cooking, before you turn them over.

MAKES 2 DOZEN 4-INCH PANCAKES

* In a large bowl, combine the flour, sugar, baking powder, and salt. In another bowl, whisk the eggs, buttermilk, milk, and melted butter until well blended. Add the egg mixture to the flour mixture and whisk just until combined.

* Heat a 10- or 12-inch cast iron skillet or a cast iron griddle over medium heat. Add 1 tablespoon vegetable oil to the skillet. Pour the batter into the skillet, ¼ cup at a time, forming small pancakes. When bubbles start to form, turn the pancakes over and cook until golden brown, 2 to 3 minutes longer. Continue until all the batter is used up, adding more vegetable oil as necessary. Serve with melted butter and warm maple syrup.

2 cups all-purpose flour

2 tablespoons sugar

2 teaspoons baking powder

½ teaspoon salt

2 eggs

2 cups buttermilk

½ cup whole milk

¼ cup (½ stick) salted butter, melted, plus additional melted butter for serving

1 tablespoon vegetable oil, plus more if needed

Warm maple syrup, for serving

tortilla española

(Spanish Potato Omelet)

Similar to a frittata, this traditional Spanish dish can be served warm or cold. A friend of ours once brought it on a ski trip, and we sat in the sun enjoying this delicious potato omelet. The dish turns out golden brown and moist, with layers of potato.

MAKES 4 SERVINGS

1 cup extra-virgin olive oil

1 medium yellow onion, thinly sliced

2 pounds Yukon Gold or russet potatoes, peeled and cut into ⅛-inch slices

Salt and freshly ground black pepper

6 eggs

¼ teaspoon smoked paprika, for garnish

2 tablespoons chopped chives or parsley, for garnish

Sour cream, for serving

Hot sauce, for serving

✳ Line a large bowl with paper towels.

✳ Heat a 10- or 12-inch cast iron skillet over medium heat. Add the olive oil. When the oil is hot, add the onions and potatoes and cook, gently flipping them occasionally. Cook until they are light golden brown, about 15 minutes. Using a slotted spoon, transfer them to a large bowl. Sprinkle with salt and pepper and set aside. Discard all but 1 tablespoon of the oil in the skillet.

✳ Break the eggs into a medium bowl and whisk well. Add the cooked potatoes and onions to the eggs. Heat the same skillet over medium heat. Add the egg-potato mixture and cook for 3 minutes, smoothing the mixture evenly with the back of a spatula.

✳ At this point, you can put the skillet in the oven under the broiler for 2 to 3 minutes to brown the top. Season with more salt and pepper, and garnish with the paprika and chives. Serve with sour cream and hot sauce alongside.

dutch baby

This is a recipe meant for the cast iron skillet. Just a few ingredients produce an amazing puffed pancake that looks as though it might rise right out of the pan. We like to serve this puffed pancake on lazy Saturday mornings and, even more, we love getting it served to us on Mother's Day.

MAKES 2 SERVINGS

* Preheat the oven to 425°F.

* To prepare the Dutch baby, melt the butter in a 12-inch cast iron skillet over low heat. Mix the eggs, flour, and milk in a blender on medium speed until just blended, 5 to 10 seconds. Pour the batter into the skillet with the melted butter.

* Place the skillet in the oven and bake until the top puffs up and is lightly golden, about 25 minutes.

* When the Dutch baby is done, drizzle the melted butter over the top, and then sprinkle with the lemon juice and dust with the powdered sugar. Cut into 6 wedges and serve immediately.

2 tablespoons butter
4 extra-large eggs
⅔ cup all-purpose flour
⅔ cup whole milk

TOPPING
2 tablespoons butter, melted
Juice of 1 lemon
½ cup powdered sugar

savory dutch baby

This recipe adds ham and cheese to the traditional Dutch baby, making a heartier variation suitable for lunch or dinner.

MAKES 2 SERVINGS

3 tablespoons butter

4 extra-large eggs

⅔ cup all-purpose flour

⅔ cup whole milk

½ cup grated Swiss or Gruyère cheese

½ cup (about three ¼-inch-thick slices) chopped ham (French, Black Forest, or honey)

✤ Preheat the oven to 425°F.

✤ To prepare the Dutch baby, melt the butter in a 12-inch cast iron skillet over low heat. Mix the eggs, flour, and milk in a blender on medium speed until just blended, 5 to 10 seconds. Pour the batter into a medium bowl, and add the cheese and ham, folding them into the mixture. Pour into the skillet with the melted butter.

✤ Place the skillet in the oven and bake until the top puffs up and is lightly golden, 20 to 25 minutes.

✤ When the Dutch baby is done, cut into 6 wedges and serve immediately.

amazing popovers

Serve these hot out of the oven with butter and strawberry jam. We also like to add 1 teaspoon fresh thyme to the batter and serve them alongside roast beef. The cast iron pan cooks the popovers evenly and results in crisp, golden treats.

MAKES 6 SERVINGS

* Preheat oven to 375°F.

* In a medium bowl, combine the flour and salt. In another bowl, whisk together the milk and eggs and stir in the butter. Gradually whisk in the flour and salt mixture. Using a pastry brush, coat the inside of the popover cups with the vegetable oil.

* Place the popover pan in the preheated oven for 5 minutes. Then remove it from the oven, and fill each popover cup with ½ cup of the batter. Return the pan to the oven and bake for 35 to 40 minutes, until the popovers are puffed and golden.

1 cup all-purpose flour
½ teaspoon salt
1 cup milk, heated to 90°F to 100°F
2 large eggs, at room temperature
1 tablespoon butter, melted
1 tablespoon vegetable oil

swedish pancakes

Light and delicious, these pancakes are not heavy "sinkers." This is another traditional recipe from our Northwest Scandinavian community. We use a cast iron Swedish pancake pan that has a small lip around the edge, making it easy to flip the pancakes, but you can use your skillet or griddle instead. We also make large 8-inch pancakes, fill them with strawberries and whipped cream, and then roll them up to serve.

MAKES 4 SERVINGS

3 extra-large eggs

2¼ cups whole milk

3 tablespoons butter, melted, plus additional for serving

1¼ cups all-purpose flour

⅛ teaspoon salt

3 to 4 tablespoons vegetable oil

Peach sauce or fresh berry syrup, for serving

Whipped cream, for serving

✳ In a large bowl, beat the eggs, milk, and melted butter. In a separate bowl, whisk together the flour and salt. Stir the wet ingredients into the dry ingredients and mix well with a whisk or electric mixer until smooth.

✳ Heat 1 teaspoon of the vegetable oil in a cast iron skillet or griddle over medium heat. Drop about ¼ cup of batter into the hot skillet for each pancake. They should be small, 3 to 4 inches across. Cook until golden brown on both sides. Repeat with the remaining oil and batter. Serve with melted butter, peach sauce, and a dollop of whipped cream.

ebelskivers

(Scandinavian Pancakes)

Ebelskivers are like little doughnuts without the fat. This recipe calls for a special cast iron pan, with seven round molds. You drop some of the batter into each mold, cook for 2 minutes, turn over and cook on the other side, and you have these amazing, golden Scandinavian treats. Ebelskivers are delicious cut in half and served with mascarpone and fresh berry jam. You can also add powdered sugar or cinnamon-sugar to a brown paper bag, place the ebelskivers inside, and shake to coat. Kids love to help with this step.

MAKES 4 TO 6 SERVINGS

1½ cups all-purpose flour
1 teaspoon baking powder
½ teaspoon baking soda
¼ teaspoon salt
2 eggs, beaten
1 cup sour cream or yogurt
½ cup milk
2 egg whites, beaten
¼ cup vegetable oil, divided

Jam or maple syrup and
    powdered sugar, for serving

* Sift the flour, baking powder, baking soda, and salt into a large bowl. In a small bowl, whisk together the eggs, sour cream, and milk. Add the egg mixture to the flour mixture and beat by hand until smooth. Fold in the egg whites.

* Heat a cast iron ebelskiver pan over medium-low heat. Place ½ teaspoon oil in each indentation, and then fill each two-thirds full with batter. Cook until light brown, about 2 minutes. Turn gently with a fork or chopstick and brown the other side. Transfer to a platter and serve with maple syrup and powdered sugar.

overnight french toast

The cast iron skillet browns and crisps French toast better than any other pan. Soaking the bread the night before makes the final result light and fluffy. Crispy, browned link sausages make a good accompaniment.

MAKES 4 SERVINGS

1 baguette, cut into 1½-inch-
  thick slices
1½ cups half-and-half
4 eggs
1 teaspoon vanilla extract
¼ cup sugar
¼ teaspoon cinnamon
⅛ teaspoon salt
2 tablespoons butter, plus more
  as needed
1 tablespoon vegetable oil, plus
  more as needed

Warm maple syrup, for serving

* Place the baguette slices in a 9 x 13-inch pan. In a medium bowl, whisk together the half-and-half, eggs, and vanilla. In a small bowl, mix the sugar, cinnamon, and salt. Whisk the sugar mixture into the egg mixture. Pour over the bread slices, turning them to coat well. Cover with plastic wrap, and refrigerate overnight. (If your time is limited, 1 hour ahead works just fine.)

* Position a rack in the center of the oven, and preheat to 350°F.

* Melt 2 tablespoons butter in a 10- or 12-inch cast iron skillet or a cast iron griddle over medium heat. Add 1 tablespoon vegetable oil. Just after the butter foams, add 6 slices of the bread and cook for 2 minutes. Turn and cook for 2 minutes longer. After the second side is golden brown, transfer to a baking sheet in the oven for 10 minutes to finish cooking. Repeat with the remaining slices of bread, adding more butter and oil to the skillet as needed for cooking. Serve on warm plates with warm maple syrup.

dungeness crab and tillamook cheddar soufflé

The combination of bread, eggs, cream, and overnight soaking results in a souf-flé-like dish. Assemble this dish the night before and refrigerate. Add the crab just before baking. Instead of using crab, you can cook 1 pound of breakfast sausages, and then cut each sausage into thirds and mix with the bread and cheese.

MAKES 8 SERVINGS

* Generously butter a 10-inch cast iron skillet. Whisk the eggs and half-and-half together in a medium bowl until well blended. In another bowl, mix together the cheese and bread cubes, and then spread evenly in the buttered skillet. Pour the egg mixture over the top. Cover and refrigerate for at least 2 hours or overnight.

* When ready to bake, position a rack in the center of the oven and preheat to 350°F. Spread the crabmeat over the eggs, and then place the skillet in the oven and bake the soufflé until puffed and lightly browned, about 50 minutes. Remove from the oven, sprinkle with parsley, cut into wedges, and serve with a fresh tomato salsa.

6 large eggs

2 cups half-and-half

2 cups grated Tillamook cheddar cheese

10 slices French bread, cut into 1-inch cubes

8 ounces Dungeness crabmeat

2 tablespoons chopped fresh parsley

Fresh tomato salsa, for serving

zucchini-onion frittata

Not just for the breakfast menu, this egg dish, which is served at room temperature, is a perfect accompaniment to roast chicken for picnics. The skillet cooks the frittata low and slow and forms a delicious crust.

MAKES 8 SERVINGS

6 tablespoons extra-virgin olive oil

1 sweet yellow onion, quartered and thinly sliced into ¼-inch crescents

9 small zucchini (2 pounds), washed, dried, halved lengthwise, and cut into ¼-inch-thick slices

1 teaspoon sea salt

Freshly ground black pepper

⅛ teaspoon freshly grated nutmeg

¼ cup fresh bread crumbs

1½ cups finely grated Parmesan cheese, divided

9 large eggs

3 tablespoons chopped fresh basil

Salsa and sour cream, for serving

❋ Position a rack in the center of the oven and preheat to 300°F.

❋ Warm 4 tablespoons of the olive oil in a 10-inch cast iron skillet over medium heat. Add the onions, stirring to coat with the olive oil, and cook for 5 minutes. Add the zucchini and stir gently to mix with the onions. Reduce the heat to low, cover, and cook until the zucchini softens, about 8 minutes.

❋ Remove from the heat, and drain off any liquid from the pan. Spread the onions and zucchini evenly in the skillet. Season with salt, pepper, and nutmeg. Sprinkle with the bread crumbs and 1 cup of the Parmesan cheese.

❋ Crack the eggs into a medium bowl and whisk until well blended. Stir in the basil. Pour over the zucchini mixture, cover the pan loosely with foil, and bake for 45 minutes.

❋ Remove the foil and sprinkle with the remaining ½ cup cheese. Raise the oven rack 3 inches. Preheat the broiler, and broil the frittata until golden brown on top, 2 to 3 minutes. Drizzle the remaining 2 tablespoons of olive oil over the frittata. Slice into wedges and serve with salsa and sour cream.

❋ If not serving right away, remove the wedges from the skillet, using a slotted spatula to drain off extra juices. Transfer to a serving platter and keep warm.

joe's special

This San Francisco specialty is a quick, easy egg dish. It might look messy, but it is delicious to eat. Serve with Tabasco sauce and crisp buttered toast. The skillet browns the meat and cooks the eggs. To clean the skillet after you're finished, soak the pan briefly, and then scour lightly with a plastic scrubbing pad.

MAKES 4 SERVINGS

* Melt the butter in a 10-inch cast iron skillet over medium heat. Add the onions and cook, stirring occasionally, until soft, 3 to 4 minutes. Sprinkle the oregano over the onions. Crumble the ground beef into the pan. Cook, stirring often, until the beef is evenly browned, 3 to 5 minutes. Add the pepper and spinach. Cook and stir until the spinach wilts. Add the Parmesan cheese and bell pepper.

* Crack the eggs carefully over the spinach-meat mixture, spacing them evenly around the dish. Cover and cook over medium-low heat for about 5 minutes, or until the whites have set and the yolks have just begun to set.

* Serve on warm plates, making sure each serving contains an egg. Sprinkle additional cheese and bell pepper over each serving. Serve with Tabasco sauce and buttered toast.

2 tablespoons butter

1 cup chopped yellow onion (about ½ onion)

1 tablespoon chopped fresh oregano, or 1 teaspoon dried oregano

¾ pound lean ground beef

½ teaspoon freshly ground black pepper

3 ounces baby spinach, coarsely chopped

½ cup grated Parmesan cheese, plus more for garnish

¼ cup chopped red bell pepper (about ¼ pepper), plus more for garnish

6 eggs

beef brisket hash

with Yukon Gold Potatoes

We love to use the cast iron skillet for this dish because we can achieve a nice golden crust. The crust scrapes away from the pan and adds flavor to the hash. Make the Slow-Roasted Beef Brisket (page 72) on Sunday, and then on Monday evening use the leftover beef brisket to make this easy and delicious hash.

MAKES 4 SERVINGS

¼ cup (½ stick) salted butter

1 cup diced yellow onion (about ½ onion)

6 cups peeled, diced, and cooked Yukon Gold potatoes (about 2 pounds)

4 cups chopped leftover beef brisket

¼ cup heavy cream

Salt and lots of freshly ground black pepper

3 tablespoons fresh chopped parsley, for garnish

Chili sauce or ketchup, for serving

❋ Melt the butter in a 10- or 12-inch cast iron skillet over medium heat. Add the onions and cook for 5 minutes. Stir in the potatoes and meat and cook for 10 minutes. Add the cream and stir gently. Be sure to scrape up the crispy crust that forms on the bottom of the pan. Cook until hot and the potatoes are nicely browned. Season to taste with salt and pepper. Sprinkle with chopped parsley. Serve with chili sauce or ketchup.

mom's amazing banana bread

The cardamom gives this banana bread a surprisingly nice flavor. The skillet makes the outside of the bread golden and crisp, while the bananas and sour cream keep the inside moist. We love to toast our banana bread and spread cream cheese over the top.

MAKES 8 SERVINGS

* Preheat the oven to 350°F. Using an electric mixer on medium-high speed, beat the butter, granulated sugar, and brown sugar in a large bowl until smooth and creamy. Beat in the eggs, one at a time, and then beat in the bananas and vanilla.

* In a separate bowl, mix together the flour, baking soda, salt, cinnamon, cardamom, and allspice. Add the flour mixture to the banana mixture and fold in with a spatula until well blended. Gently fold the nuts and sour cream into the batter until just blended, being careful not to overmix.

* Lightly butter a 10- or 12-inch cast iron skillet. Pour the batter into the skillet, and then place in the oven and bake until a toothpick inserted in the center comes out clean, 45 minutes to 1 hour.

* Remove from the oven and let cool in the pan. To serve, you can either flip the bread out of the pan or serve it in the skillet, sliced into wedges.

½ cup (1 stick) unsalted butter, at room temperature
½ cup granulated sugar
½ cup packed light brown sugar
2 eggs
3 overripe bananas, well mashed
½ teaspoon vanilla extract
2 cups all-purpose flour
1 teaspoon baking soda
¼ teaspoon salt
½ teaspoon ground cinnamon
½ teaspoon ground cardamom
Dash ground allspice
¼ cup chopped pecans or walnuts
¼ cup sour cream

buttermilk breakfast scones

with Dried Currants

These traditional flaky scones are delicious split in half and topped with sweet butter and fresh raspberry jam.

MAKES 1 DOZEN SCONES

SCONES

3 cups unbleached all-purpose flour
⅓ cup sugar
2⅓ teaspoons baking powder
½ teaspoon baking soda
¾ teaspoon salt
¾ cup (1½ sticks) chilled butter, cut into 6 to 8 pieces
½ cup dried currants
1 teaspoon grated orange zest
1 cup buttermilk

GLAZE

1 tablespoon heavy cream
¼ teaspoon ground cinnamon
2 tablespoons sugar

* Position a rack in the center of the oven and preheat to 400°F.

* To prepare the scones, stir the flour, sugar, baking powder, baking soda, and salt together in a large bowl. Add the butter and beat with an electric mixer just until blended. Add the currants and orange zest. Pour in the buttermilk and mix just until blended.

* Gather the dough into a ball. On a lightly floured board, roll the dough out into a circle, approximately ½ to ¾ inch thick. Cut the circle into 12 wedges.

* Place the scones in a circle, ½ inch apart, in a well-buttered 12-inch cast iron skillet, and bake until golden, 20 to 25 minutes. Remove from the oven.

* While the scones are baking, prepare the glaze, combining the cream, cinnamon, and sugar in a small bowl. After removing the scones from the oven, brush with the glaze and serve.

brown sugar and blueberry coffee cake

Nothing looks better on a Sunday morning than a warm coffee cake, still in the skillet, in the center of the kitchen table. The sour cream makes it moist and perfectly balances the crisp walnuts, cinnamon, and brown sugar on top.

MAKES 12 SERVINGS

* Grease a 12-inch cast iron skillet with 1 tablespoon of the butter. Position a rack in the center of the oven and preheat to 350°F.

* To prepare the cake, put the butter in a large mixing bowl. Add the brown sugar and beat with an electric mixer until light and fluffy. Add the eggs, one at a time, beating after each addition. Add the vanilla and sour cream, and stir with a spatula to combine.

* In a separate bowl, mix together the flour and baking powder, and then fold into the butter mixture until completely blended. Spread the batter evenly in the prepared skillet.

* Sprinkle the blueberries over the top, gently pressing them into the batter.

* To prepare the topping, mix together the flour, brown sugar, cinnamon, walnuts, and chilled butter with your fingers until evenly blended. Sprinkle evenly over the cake batter. Place the skillet in the oven and bake for 35 to 40 minutes. When you gently touch the center of the cake with your fingers, it should feel firm to your touch. Serve warm.

CAKE

1 cup (2 sticks) salted butter, at room temperature, plus 1 tablespoon for greasing the pan
1 cup packed light brown sugar
2 large eggs
1 teaspoon vanilla extract
¾ cup sour cream
2½ cups all-purpose flour
1½ teaspoons baking powder
2 cups blueberries

TOPPING

½ cup all-purpose flour
¾ cup packed light brown sugar
1 teaspoon ground cinnamon
1 cup chopped walnuts or pecans
6 tablespoons chilled butter, cut into 4 pieces

grandmother kramis's irish soda bread

The cast iron skillet works wonders for Irish Soda Bread. That's how our Irish grandmother made it, and that's how we've always done it too. We break a wedge in half and spread it with the Whipped Orange Butter before settling down with a cup of hot tea.

MAKES 8 SERVINGS

4 cups all-purpose flour

1 teaspoon baking soda

2 teaspoons baking powder

½ cup sugar

½ cup currants, or 1 cup raisins

Pinch salt

½ cup (1 stick) unsalted butter, melted

2 eggs

2 cups buttermilk

Whipped Orange Butter (see note), for serving

❦ Position a rack in the center of the oven and preheat to 350°F.

❦ In a large bowl, mix together the flour, baking soda, baking powder, sugar, currants, and salt. In a small bowl, whisk together the butter, eggs, and buttermilk. Pour the butter mixture into the flour mixture, and stir with a spoon until it forms a dough. Place the dough onto a lightly floured surface and knead until well combined. Butter a 10-inch cast iron skillet and place the dough in the skillet, flattening it to fill the bottom of the pan. Score a large X across the top of the dough. Bake until a toothpick inserted in the center of the bread comes out clean, 25 to 30 minutes.

NOTE: To prepare the Whipped Orange Butter, whip softened butter with a whisk until it is light and fluffy. Whisk in grated orange zest to taste and spread on the soda bread.

pecan sticky buns

The cast iron skillet heats so evenly that these rolls come out golden brown, with an amazing caramel sauce on the bottom. Serve the buns right from the skillet or invert them onto a serving plate. They are sticky and irresistible.

MAKES 1 DOZEN ROLLS

✴ To prepare the dough, dissolve the yeast in the warm water in a mixing bowl. Let rest for 5 minutes. Add ½ cup of the flour, the granulated sugar, salt, vanilla, milk, and eggs to the yeast mixture. In a mixing bowl with dough hook attachment, mix on low speed or by hand until blended. Slowly add the remaining flour and mix well. Add the butter and knead or mix with dough hook until butter is incorporated and dough is smooth. Place in a well-greased bowl, cover with plastic wrap, and let rise until doubled in size, about 45 minutes. Punch down dough, knead a couple times, cover, and allow to double again in a warm place for 4 hours.

✴ While the dough rises, prepare the glaze. Place the brown sugar, butter, honey, corn syrup, and water in an 8- or 10-inch cast iron skillet and mix well. Place the skillet over medium heat and cook, without stirring, until the butter is melted and the liquid is bubbling, about 5 minutes. Sprinkle the pecans evenly over the glaze, remove from the heat, and let cool.

✴ Remove dough from bowl and transfer to a lightly floured surface. Roll the dough into a 10 x 15-inch rectangle. To prepare the filling, mix together the cinnamon, nutmeg, granulated sugar, and raisins. Spread the softened butter over the dough, and sprinkle the dough with the sugar-raisin mixture. Roll up like a jelly roll (starting from the 15-inch side), and then cut into 1½-inch slices by sliding a

(continued)

DOUGH

1 package dry yeast
¼ cup warm water
2½ cups all-purpose flour
⅓ cup granulated sugar
1 teaspoon salt
1 teaspoon vanilla extract
¼ cup milk
2 eggs
6 tablespoons unsalted butter, at room temperature

GLAZE

⅔ cup packed light brown sugar
6 tablespoons unsalted butter, at room temperature
3 tablespoons honey
3 tablespoons dark corn syrup
3 tablespoons water
1 cup pecan halves, coarsely chopped

FILLING

2 teaspoons ground cinnamon
¼ teaspoon freshly grated nutmeg
½ cup granulated sugar
2 cups raisins, softened in hot water and drained (optional)
¼ cup (½ stick) unsalted butter, softened

thread under the roll, crossing the ends over the top, and pulling tight. (This way the dough isn't compressed.) Place the slices flat on top of the glaze in the skillet, and let them rise for 30 minutes.

* While the buns are rising, position a rack in the center of the oven and preheat to 375°F.

* Bake the buns for 20 to 25 minutes, until golden brown and firm to the touch. Protecting both hands with oven mitts, grasp the skillet and carefully turn sticky buns onto a slightly larger plate. Serve warm.

APPETIZERS

hese recipes for appetizers offer a melting pot of flavors from around the world. Queso Fundido Verde, served hot and bubbling in the skillet, is a warm centerpiece that everyone likes to gather around. The Eggplant-Pepper Tapenade brings a taste of the Mediterranean to your table and is a perfect dish to serve with other appetizers. We love the sweet and spicy flavors of the Asian Beef, and the lettuce wraps are a fun presentation. Quesadillas are a good example of how you can use your cast iron skillet to quickly create an afternoon snack or a pre-dinner appetizer. Although these appetizers are made to order, you can have them ready ahead of time, and then cook them and serve them hot to your guests.

grilled prosciutto-wrapped radicchio

with Balsamic Vinegar and Olive Oil

The radicchio's bitterness, the prosciutto's saltiness, and the balsamic vinegar's tart sweetness perform the perfect balancing act, resulting in a flavor combination that practically explodes in your mouth. Use an aged balsamic vinegar for a less acidic flavor. If you use a young balsamic, reduce it over medium heat until it begins to thicken; you can also add a bit of sugar for extra sweetness.

MAKES 8 SERVINGS

* Wrap each piece of radicchio tightly with a slice of prosciutto.

* Divide the radicchio into two batches. Heat 2 tablespoons of the olive oil in a 10- or 12-inch cast iron skillet over medium-high heat. Place the first batch of wrapped radicchio in the pan, and sear on all sides until the prosciutto browns and the radicchio starts to soften and changes to a deeper burgundy color, about 5 minutes. Transfer to a plate. Repeat with the remaining olive oil and the second batch of wrapped radicchio.

* Drizzle the radicchio with the balsamic vinegar and season with freshly ground black pepper. Serve immediately.

3 small heads radicchio, each cut into six wedges
8 to 10 slices prosciutto, sliced in half lengthwise
4 tablespoons extra-virgin olive oil, divided
¼ cup balsamic vinegar
Freshly ground black pepper

queso fundido verde

Seattle's Cactus restaurant is one of our favorites because they use great ingredients and combine amazing flavors. They shared their recipe for Queso Fundido Verde with us because it works so well in an iron skillet. This dish turns out like a Mexican version of fondue, with chorizo sausage crumbled over the top. You can also heat and serve this dish in four 4-inch skillets: just place 1 cup of the fundido mixture into each skillet and broil for 3 to 5 minutes. Serve with tortilla chips and, of course, margaritas!

MAKES 4 SERVINGS

2 poblano chiles
8 ounces chorizo sausage
2½ cups (20 ounces) cream cheese, at room temperature
1 cup mayonnaise
½ cup finely chopped green onion, plus additional for garnish
½ cup chopped white onion
2 teaspoons minced garlic
2⅔ cups grated Jack cheese
1 cup crumbled feta cheese
¾ cup fresh or frozen corn (thawed and drained if frozen)
½ cup diced red bell pepper

1 lime, quartered, for garnish
Tortilla chips, for serving

✻ To roast the poblano chiles, place them directly over the flame of a gas stove or in a cast iron skillet over medium-high heat. Roast, turning occasionally, until the skin blackens, about 10 minutes. Transfer to a paper bag for 10 minutes to loosen the skin and cool the chiles. Remove from the bag and wipe with a damp paper towel to remove the skin. Make a cut in each chile to release the steam, and then halve them, remove the stem and seeds, and dice into ⅜-inch pieces.

✻ To prepare the chorizo, push the meat out of the casing. Heat a cast iron skillet over medium heat. Add the chorizo, breaking the meat apart with a wooden spoon. Cook, stirring occasionally, until the fat cooks out of the sausage and the sausage turns golden brown, about 5 minutes. Transfer to a bowl using a slotted spoon and set aside.

✻ Position a rack at the top of the oven and preheat to 400°F.

✻ To prepare the fundido, place the cream cheese in a large bowl and mix with an electric mixer or by hand until smooth. Scrape down the sides of the bowl with a spatula. Add the mayonnaise and mix until smooth and free of lumps. Add the green onion, white onion, garlic, Jack cheese, feta, corn, bell pepper, and roasted poblano chiles to the cream cheese mixture. Mix until well combined.

✴ Place the cream cheese mixture in an 8-inch cast iron skillet. Bake for 10 minutes, until the edges are bubbling and the top is beginning to brown. Garnish with the chorizo, chopped green onions, and a lime wedge. Serve in the skillet with a big bowl of tortilla chips.

asian beef

with Lettuce Wraps and Sweet Chili Sauce

The wonderful Slanted Door restaurant in San Francisco inspired this recipe. The sugars in the marinade caramelize beautifully when you brown the beef in an iron skillet, and the lettuce adds a fresh crunch. If you'd like, set out the warm cooked beef, lettuce leaves, bell peppers, sprouts, cilantro, basil, and Sweet Chili Sauce, and then let your guests assemble their own wraps.

MAKES 12 SERVINGS

* Position a rack in the center of the oven and preheat to 250°F.

* To prepare the sauce, whisk together the chili sauce, garlic, rice wine vinegar, serrano chile, fish sauce, and lime juice in a medium bowl. Set aside.

* To prepare the vinaigrette, whisk together the oil, rice wine vinegar, sugar, soy sauce, and fish sauce in a separate bowl. Set aside. Arrange the lettuce leaves on a large platter, cover with a damp paper towel, and refrigerate until needed.

* To prepare the beef, mix together the sugar, garlic, ginger, salt, and pepper in a large bowl. Add the beef and mix well to coat.

* Divide the beef into three batches for cooking (or else it will stew instead of brown). Place a 10- or 12-inch cast iron skillet over medium-high heat and melt ½ tablespoon of butter per batch of beef (do not crowd the pan). Add the first batch of beef, browning on both sides. Then add 2 tablespoons of the vinaigrette, turning quickly, until cooked to medium rare, about 3 minutes. Transfer the meat to a plate, and keep it warm in the oven. Wipe out skillet and repeat

(continued)

SWEET CHILI SAUCE
1 tablespoon Thai sweet chili sauce
1 clove garlic, thinly sliced
¼ cup rice wine vinegar
½ serrano chile, seeded and thinly sliced
2 tablespoons fish sauce
2 tablespoons fresh lime juice

VINAIGRETTE
2 tablespoons canola oil
½ cup rice wine vinegar
2 tablespoons sugar
¼ cup soy sauce
2 tablespoons fish sauce
12 medium Bibb lettuce leaves

BEEF
2 tablespoons sugar
2 cloves garlic, minced
1 teaspoon peeled minced fresh ginger
Salt and freshly ground black pepper
1½ pounds top sirloin or filet mignon, trimmed and cut into ¾-inch cubes

1½ tablespoons butter, divided
½ lime

WRAPS
½ red bell pepper, seeds and
   ribs removed, and cut lengthwise into ¼-inch strips
1½ cups mung bean sprouts
   (optional)
12 fresh Thai basil sprigs,
   coarsely chopped
12 fresh cilantro sprigs

1 tablespoon unsalted peanuts,
   finely chopped, for garnish
Sriracha sauce, for serving

with the other two batches of meat. After all the meat is browned, squeeze the lime juice over the top.

✢ To assemble, place a few pieces of beef inside a lettuce leaf with a couple of strips of bell pepper, some bean sprouts, ½ teaspoon basil, and a sprig of cilantro. Drizzle with a little chili sauce, sprinkle with some peanuts, and roll up. Repeat with the remaining lettuce leaves and enjoy! Serve with Sriracha sauce on the side.

wild mushroom crostini and chèvre

In the Pacific Northwest, where we live, chanterelles come up after the first rain in September. You can make the crostini up to several days ahead. Reheat and spoon on the warm mushroom topping when you are ready to serve.

MAKES 8 SERVINGS

* Position a rack in the center of the oven and preheat to 375°F.

* To prepare the crostini, place the baguette slices on a baking sheet. Brush the top side of each slice with the olive oil. Sprinkle with the herbs de Provence and bake until crisp, 12 to 15 minutes. Remove from the oven and let cool on the baking sheet. (If you are not using the crostini immediately, cool completely and store in a resealable plastic bag.)

* Meanwhile, coarsely chop the mushrooms into ½-inch pieces. Warm the butter in a 10- or 12-inch cast iron skillet over medium heat. Add the mushrooms and cook for 5 minutes, stirring occasionally. Reduce the heat to medium-low and cook 5 minutes longer. Add the thyme, rosemary, and Worcestershire and cook for 3 minutes, stirring occasionally. Season to taste with salt and pepper and sprinkle with the chopped parsley.

* To serve, spread each crostini with chèvre and top with warm mushrooms.

CROSTINI
1 French baguette, cut into
    ½-inch-thick slices
½ cup extra-virgin olive oil
2 tablespoons dried herbs de
    Provence

MUSHROOM TOPPING
1 pound chanterelle mushrooms,
    cleaned
2 tablespoons butter
1 teaspoon fresh thyme leaves
1 teaspoon chopped fresh
    rosemary
1 tablespoon Worcestershire
    sauce
Salt and freshly ground black
    pepper
¼ cup finely chopped parsley

6 ounces chèvre

crispy lamb skewers

with Cucumber-Tomato Relish

These tasty little lamb sausages get nice and crisp on the outside. Served hot, they are a great way to enjoy ground lamb. They don't taste gamy or greasy! Serve with tzatziki and hummus dips and pita wedges.

MAKES 12 SKEWERS

CUCUMBER-TOMATO RELISH

1 cucumber, peeled and cut into ¼-inch dice

2 tomatoes, halved, seeded, and cut into ¼-inch dice

¼ cup crumbled feta cheese

2 tablespoons olive oil

1 tablespoon red wine vinegar

LAMB

1 pound ground lamb

½ teaspoon paprika

½ teaspoon ground cumin

1 teaspoon ground coriander

2 cloves garlic, minced

Salt and freshly ground black pepper

2 tablespoons finely chopped parsley (about 5 sprigs)

12 skewers

2 pitas

Tzatziki sauce, for serving

Hummus, for serving

* In a medium bowl, mix together the cucumber, tomatoes, feta, olive oil, and vinegar. Set aside.

* In a large bowl, mix together the lamb, paprika, cumin, coriander, and garlic. Season with salt and pepper. Using about 3 tablespoons of the mixture each time, form into small sausage shapes. You should have about 12 "sausages."

* Divide the sausages into two batches. Heat a 10- or 12-inch cast iron skillet over medium-high heat, and cook the first batch, turning occasionally, until golden brown on all sides, 6 to 8 minutes. Transfer to a paper towel. Repeat with the second batch.

* Place the chopped parsley in a shallow dish, roll the lamb sausages in the parsley to coat, and skewer each sausage down the middle. Transfer to a serving dish.

* Wipe the skillet with a paper towel and place over medium heat. Warm each pita until light brown and slice into 6 wedges. Spread tzatziki or hummus on the pita wedges, and then place the lamb sausages on top. Top with the salad.

dungeness crab quesadillas

with Avocado-Lime Sauce

The iron skillet is the best way to cook quesadillas quickly and evenly. We love quesadillas cut into wedges and served as an appetizer or a quick lunch. You can cook cheese quesadillas in your skillet over a campfire or outdoor grill and serve with the Avocado-Lime Sauce.

MAKES 8 SERVINGS

* To prepare the sauce, place the avocado, lime juice, lemon juice, and sour cream in a blender and purée until smooth. Refrigerate until ready to serve. (You can prepare the sauce up to 1 hour in advance.)

* Position a rack in the center of the oven and preheat to 200°F.

* To prepare the quesadillas, mix together the crabmeat, cheese, bell pepper, green onions, mayonnaise, and lemon juice in a large bowl. Lay out 4 of the tortillas and spread evenly with the crab mixture. Top with the remaining tortillas.

* Warm a 10- or 12-inch cast iron skillet over medium-low heat. Place a quesadilla in the skillet and cook for 2 minutes, until the tortilla starts to brown, and then turn and cook on the other side until the cheese melts and the filling is warm. Transfer to a platter and keep warm in the oven. Repeat with the remaining quesadillas.

* Cut the quesadillas into wedges and drizzle lightly with the sauce. Serve on small plates with sliced avocado and lime wedges.

AVOCADO-LIME SAUCE
1 ripe avocado, peeled and
   chopped
Juice of 1 lime
1 tablespoon lemon juice
1 cup sour cream

QUESADILLAS
8 ounces Dungeness crabmeat
1 cup grated cheddar cheese
½ cup diced red bell pepper
¼ cup chopped green onion
½ cup mayonnaise
1 teaspoon fresh lemon juice
8 flour tortillas, 8 inches in
   diameter

Avocado slices, for garnish
Lime wedges, for garnish

golden fried oysters

The plumpest oysters are available in months that have an *r* in them. March is the best month. You can shuck your own oysters or buy them preshucked in jars at seafood markets. Look for the extra-small size. We love to make oyster po' boys with these crispy morsels. Just buy a crunchy baguette and lettuce and serve with the Sriracha and tartar sauces.

MAKES 8 SERVINGS

✳ To prepare the dipping sauce, whisk together the mayonnaise, lemon juice, Sriracha, and sesame oil in a small bowl. Refrigerate until ready to serve.

✳ To prepare the oysters, in a medium bowl, combine the flour, cornmeal, chili powder, salt, and pepper. Mix well with a whisk and set aside.

✳ When you are ready to cook the oysters, heat the oil in a 10- or 12-inch cast iron skillet until the temperature reads 350°F on a deep-fry thermometer. (You can also test the heat by sprinkling a small bit of flour into the oil; it should bubble immediately.)

✳ Dredge the oysters in the flour mixture, shake off the excess flour, and carefully place 6 at a time in the hot oil. (You can also use a slotted spoon or a deep-fryer basket to lower them into the oil.) Fry until golden brown, about 2 minutes. Transfer to paper towels. Repeat with the remaining oysters. Serve hot with your choice of dipping sauces.

SRIRACHA DIPPING SAUCE
½ cup mayonnaise
1 teaspoon fresh lemon juice
1 tablespoon Sriracha sauce
½ teaspoon sesame oil

OYSTERS
1 cup all-purpose flour
1 cup medium-ground yellow cornmeal
¼ teaspoon chili powder
¼ teaspoon salt
¼ teaspoon freshly ground black pepper
1 cup peanut or canola oil
24 extra-small oysters, preshucked and drained in a colander (don't rinse)

Tartar sauce (see page 102), for serving

garlic-spiced prawns

We find that when we purchase prawns with their shells on, they retain more of their true flavor. If you prefer, you can use shelled and deveined prawns. If you do keep the tails on, provide your guests with a bowl for the tails and plenty of napkins. You don't have to marinate the prawns, but they are more flavorful if you do.

MAKES 4 SERVINGS

¼ teaspoon ground turmeric
⅛ teaspoon cayenne
½ teaspoon ground coriander
½ teaspoon paprika
¼ teaspoon curry powder
2 teaspoons fresh thyme leaves,
   lightly chopped
⅛ teaspoon salt
Grated zest of 1 lemon
1 teaspoon sugar
5 tablespoons butter
2 cloves garlic, minced
1 pound medium-sized prawns,
   heads and shells removed,
   tails attached
1 tablespoon lemon or lime juice

Lettuce leaves, for serving
Lemon slices, for garnish
1 tablespoon chopped flat-leaf
   parsley, for garnish

* In a small bowl, mix together the turmeric, cayenne, coriander, paprika, curry powder, thyme, salt, lemon zest, and sugar. In a 10- or 12-inch cast iron skillet, melt the butter over low heat. Stir in the spice mixture and garlic. Increase the heat to medium-low and cook for 1 minute.

* Add the prawns to the skillet and cook for 2 to 3 minutes; turn all the prawns over and cook for 2 minutes more. Sprinkle the lemon juice over the prawns. Transfer to a large platter lined with lettuce leaves, garnish with lemon slices and parsley, and serve.

eggplant-pepper tapenade

Known as *zaalouk* in Morocco and shared with us by our friend Meriem Atowani Kass, this tapenade is traditionally served as a side dish to chicken with pre-served lemons. (See page 91 for our version using Cornish game hens.) You can also serve this as an appetizer or add it to tomato sauce and toss with pasta.

MAKES 6 TO 8 SERVINGS (ABOUT 2 CUPS)

1 red or green bell pepper
1 tablespoon extra-virgin olive oil
1 tablespoon canola oil
1 large eggplant, peeled and cut into ½-inch cubes
3 cloves garlic, minced
1 tablespoon chopped fresh cilantro
1 teaspoon paprika
¼ teaspoon salt

Warm pitas, for serving

* To roast the bell pepper, place it directly on the burner on a gas stove over medium-high heat or in a cast iron skillet over medium-high heat. Roast, turning occasionally, until the skin blackens, about 10 minutes. Transfer to a paper bag for 10 minutes to loosen the skin and cool the pepper. Remove from the bag and wipe the pepper with a damp paper towel to remove the skin. Make a cut in the pepper to release the steam. Slice in half; remove the stem, seeds, and white vein; and then cut into ½-inch cubes.

* Warm the olive oil and canola oil in a 10- or 12-inch cast iron skillet over medium-low heat. Add the roasted pepper, eggplant, garlic, cilantro, paprika, and salt and cook, stirring occasionally, for 30 minutes. The eggplant will release all of its liquid, and the mixture will become a thick sauce. Remove from the heat and serve with warmed pitas.

ENTRÉES

(continued)

Cooking in a cast iron skillet goes hand in hand with bringing everyone to the table together. Family and friends inspired many of our recipes, and many of them we created together, side by side in the kitchen, doing what we love most—preparing foods meant to be shared with loved ones. The Slow-Roasted Beef Brisket with Apple Cider–Ginger Barbecue Sauce and the Schultz Sunday Supper Pot Roast are perfect for long, leisurely weekend evenings. On busy week-nights quick, tasty meals are best: we love to serve our family Open-Face Sloppy Joes, Tom's Brick Chicken, or Pan-Seared Wild King Salmon. For special meals we enjoy Seared Beef Tenderloin with Veal Demi-Glace, Chicken Paillards with Red and Yellow Peppers and Kalamata Olives, or the wonderfully delicious and fun to eat Garlic Roasted Dungeness Crab. Whatever the occasion, when you have good food hot out of a cast iron skillet, you have a meal to share and remember.

The following cooking methods respond best to cast iron's dry, even heat.

BRAISING AND STEWING are ideal for the tough muscle cuts of meat, such as chuck roast, short ribs, shanks, shoulder meat, and stew meat. It is important to brown the meat first and then add the amount of liquid specified in the recipe. The browning and caramelizing of the outside of the meat is best done in a heated cast iron pan with a little oil or butter.

PAN-SEARING in a cast iron skillet creates a flavorful brown crust on tender cuts of meat such as pork chops, steaks, and pork tenderloins or fish fillets. To pan-sear, season the meat or fish with salt and pepper. Heat the skillet over medium-high heat, add a little olive oil, and sear both sides of the meat in the skillet. Then place the skillet with the meat or fish into a preheated 375°F oven and finish cooking according to the recipe. When pan-searing fish, scallops, skinless chicken, or pork, wait until a golden crust forms. If you force any of these prematurely from the pan, they will stick.

BROWNING in cast iron prevents excess moisture from developing. Ground beef actually browns and crisps, rather than stewing and becoming flavorless and gray as it does in other types of pans. If the only thing you do is brown ground beef in your cast iron pan, you'll be happy you have it.

STIR-FRYING works best over medium-high heat. Be sure to have all of your ingredients chopped, sliced, and diced, and ready to add to your hot skillet. Heat the pan over medium-high heat, and then add your oil, swirling it around to distribute evenly. You want to keep your ingredients moving around in the pan continuously, using a wooden spatula or tongs. Sautéing in an iron skillet browns and caramelizes meats and vegetables beautifully. For gas or electric stove top ranges, a 12- or 14-inch flat-bottomed skillet can substitute for a wok.

SAUTÉING is a gentle approach to cooking, using medium heat. As with stir-frying, sautéing in an iron skillet browns and caramelizes meats and vegetables perfectly.

lamb chops

with Pomegranate Glaze

The tartness of the pomegranate molasses is balanced by the honey in the marinade, which mellows the strong flavor lamb can sometimes have. The lamb chops sear beautifully and cook quickly in the iron skillet. Serve with couscous and roasted vegetables.

MAKES 4 SERVINGS

* Position a rack in the center of the oven and preheat to 350°F.

* In a medium bowl, mix together the pomegranate molasses, honey, red wine, ¼ cup olive oil, garlic, and coriander. Place the rib chops in a 9 x 12-inch glass baking dish, pour the marinade over the top, and sprinkle with salt and pepper. Cover with plastic wrap and refrigerate for 2 to 3 hours, turning the chops over a couple of times.

* Heat 1 tablespoon of the remaining olive oil in a 10- or 12-inch cast iron skillet over medium-high heat. Working in batches of 4 chops at a time, brown the chops on both sides, adding another 1 tablespoon oil for each batch. Transfer to a baking sheet. Repeat with the remaining two batches.

* When all of the chops are on the baking sheet, place it in the oven and bake for 10 minutes for medium-rare or 15 minutes for medium. Remove from the oven, cover the chops with foil, and let the meat rest for 5 minutes.

* To serve, place 3 chops on each plate.

¼ cup pomegranate molasses (see note)
¼ cup honey
½ cup red wine
¼ cup plus 3 tablespoons extra-virgin olive oil
2 cloves garlic, minced
1 teaspoon ground coriander
12 individual lamb rib chops (buy 6 two-rib chops and cut them in half)
Salt and freshly ground black pepper

NOTE: Pomegranate molasses is available at specialty grocery stores.

rosemary-crusted rack of lamb

The rack is the rib section of the lamb. There are usually seven or eight rib bones. In this recipe two racks of lamb are cooked in the oven and then sliced into individual chops. It's hard to resist the temptation to pick up the lamb chops to get every bite of meat. Serve the lamb with oven-roasted potatoes and spring asparagus.

MAKES 4 SERVINGS

* Position a rack in the center of the oven and preheat to 350°F.

* In a medium bowl, mix together the bread crumbs, rosemary, parsley, garlic, and melted butter. Set aside.

* If the rack of lamb has not been trimmed, make sure to trim the fat in between the bones and score the fat, lightly cutting diagonally with a crisscross pattern. Season the racks of lamb with salt and pepper. Place them in a 12-inch cast iron skillet, meat side up, interlocking both sets of ribs in the center of the skillet. Cover the bone ends with pieces of foil, and place the pan in the oven. Partially close the oven door and broil for 8 to 10 minutes.

* Remove the pan from the oven, and reduce the heat to 325°F. Brush each rack with 1 tablespoon Dijon mustard. Spread the bread crumb mixture evenly over both racks. Return the pan to the oven, but this time place it on the middle rack and roast for 20 to 25 minutes. Remove from the oven, cover the rack loosely with foil, and let rest for 3 to 5 minutes. Cut in between rib bones, and serve each person 3 to 4 lamb chops. Serve with hot pepper jelly or fresh mint sauce.

1¼ cups fresh white bread crumbs

1 tablespoon chopped fresh rosemary

1 tablespoon chopped fresh parsley

2 cloves garlic, minced

¼ cup (½ stick) salted butter, melted

2 racks standard domestic lamb, trimmed of all fat

Salt and freshly ground black pepper

2 tablespoons Dijon mustard

Hot pepper jelly or fresh mint sauce, for serving

stir-fried flank steak

The cast iron skillet acts just like a wok and caramelizes the beef strips in this Asian-style dish with flavors of soy and ginger. Have all of your ingredients ready before cooking. Keeping the food moving in the pan is the secret to a successful stir-fry.

MAKES 4 SERVINGS

5 tablespoons soy sauce

5 tablespoons orange juice

2 cloves garlic, peeled and minced

½ teaspoon crushed red pepper flakes

2 teaspoons fresh ginger, peeled and grated

2 teaspoons Chinese five-spice powder

1 teaspoon cornstarch

¼ cup sugar

2 teaspoons sesame oil

1 pound flank steak

2 tablespoons vegetable oil

½ red bell pepper, seeds and ribs removed and cut into ½-inch strips

½ yellow bell pepper, seeds and ribs removed, cut into ¼-inch strips

½ red onion, cut crosswise into ¼-inch crescent slices

4 ounces sugar snap peas, cut in half at an angle

Steamed rice, for serving

* To prepare the sauce, in a small bowl, combine the first 9 ingredients (soy sauce through sesame oil) and set aside.

* Cut the flank steak in half lengthwise, and then cut diagonally, crosswise, into ½-inch-wide strips.

* Warm the vegetable oil in a 12-inch cast iron skillet over medium-high heat. Add the beef strips and stir-fry for 2 minutes. Add the bell peppers, onion, and peas. Stir-fry for 1 minute. Add the sauce mixture and stir-fry until the sauce starts to bubble, about 2 minutes more. Serve immediately over steamed rice.

monday night meatloaf

This recipe makes enough for a weekend family dinner, sandwiches the next day, and meatloaf hash for a weeknight dinner.

MAKES 8 SERVINGS

* Position a rack in the center of the oven and preheat to 350°F.

* In a 10- or 12-inch cast iron skillet, melt the butter over medium heat. Stir in the chopped onion and cook for 3 minutes. Transfer to a large mixing bowl. Place all of the remaining ingredients in the bowl with the onions, and mix together with your hands until well blended. Form into a football-shaped loaf in the same skillet in which you cooked the onions.

* Place the skillet in the oven and bake until the center is no longer pink, about 1 hour. Let cool for 10 minutes. Pour off the excess fat and juices. Slice and serve hot, with ketchup for dipping.

2 tablespoons salted butter
1 cup chopped yellow onion
   (about 1 medium onion)
1 cup fresh bread crumbs
1 pound extra-lean ground beef
½ pound ground pork
1 (8-ounce) can tomato sauce
1 tablespoon Worcestershire
   sauce
2 large eggs
1 cup grated cheddar cheese
1 teaspoon salt
½ teaspoon freshly ground
   black pepper
2 teaspoons dried Italian herb
   seasoning

Ketchup, for serving

seared beef tenderloin

with Veal Demi-Glace

Demi-glace is a highly concentrated, flavorful meat sauce used as a base. Making a demi-glace would normally take all day, but when we discovered premade demi-glaces, that problem was solved. These demi-glaces are the real thing, rich and flavorful. Serve this at a dinner party and your guests will feel very special. Try it with mashed potatoes or polenta to soak up the sauce, along with green beans or Skillet-Roasted Asparagus (page 129).

MAKES 4 SERVINGS

SAUCE

2 tablespoons unsalted butter, divided

1 tablespoon finely chopped shallots

¾ ounce veal demi-glace (see Resources, page 189)

¼ cup water

¼ cup red wine

2 tablespoons marsala wine or port

1 bay leaf

Salt and freshly ground black pepper

4 (8-ounce) beef tenderloin fillets

Salt and freshly ground black pepper

1 tablespoon extra-virgin olive oil

＊ Position a rack in the center of the oven and preheat to 350°F.

＊ To prepare the sauce, melt 1 tablespoon of the butter in a small saucepan over medium-low heat. Add the shallots and cook, stirring occasionally, until softened, about 3 minutes. Reduce the heat to low. Whisk in the demi-glace and the water, stirring until the demi-glace has dissolved. Whisk in the wine, marsala, bay leaf, salt, and pepper. Remove from the heat and whisk in the remaining tablespoon of butter. Reheat just before serving.

＊ To prepare the steaks, season on both sides with salt and pepper. Warm the olive oil in a 10- or 12-inch cast iron skillet over medium-high heat for 2 minutes. Add the steaks and sear on each side until golden brown, about 3 minutes per side. Transfer the skillet to the oven and cook for 10 minutes for medium-rare, 15 minutes for medium.

＊ Remove the skillet from the oven. Remove steaks from the pan and cover loosely with aluminum foil. Let stand for

5 minutes. Remove the bay leaf from the sauce. Transfer the steaks to plates, and pour some sauce over each one. (You can pour the sauce through a small sieve first if you prefer to leave out the shallots.)

braised spareribs in merlot sauce

This recipe was inspired by our friend Frank Wesner, who uses beef short ribs. We decided to try a leaner version using the country-style spareribs. There is no need for a knife—the meat is fork tender and melts in your mouth. For the canned tomatoes, we like Muir Glen fire-roasted tomatoes for their depth of flavor. Serve these ribs with Horseradish Mashed Potatoes (recipe follows).

MAKES 6 SERVINGS

3 pounds country-style pork spareribs
Salt and freshly ground black pepper

MERLOT SAUCE
1 medium yellow onion, coarsely chopped (about 1 cup)
6 to 8 cloves garlic, coarsely chopped
2 (14.5-ounce) cans Muir Glen fire-roasted crushed tomatoes (see note, page 71) or regular crushed tomatoes (drain off excess liquid)
¼ cup packed light brown sugar
1 cup merlot or other full-bodied red wine
⅔ cup balsamic vinegar
½ teaspoon salt
½ teaspoon freshly ground black pepper

❋ Position a rack in the center of the oven and preheat to 350°F.

❋ To prepare the ribs, rinse them, pat dry with a paper towel, and season with salt and pepper on both sides. Place a 12-inch cast iron skillet over medium-high heat; add the ribs, fat side down. Cook, turning once, until browned on all sides, 2 to 3 minutes. Transfer the ribs to a plate, and then drain and reserve all but 2 tablespoons of fat from the skillet.

❋ To prepare the sauce, turn down the heat to medium-low, add the onions to the skillet, and cook, stirring occasionally, until they start to soften, about 5 minutes. Add the garlic and cook for 2 minutes. Stir in the tomatoes, brown sugar, red wine, balsamic vinegar, salt, and pepper.

❋ Turn the heat up to medium, and bring the sauce to a boil. Return the spareribs to the skillet, pushing them down gently to submerge. Protecting both hands with oven mitts, cover the skillet tightly with foil. The liquid will reduce while cooking, leaving a rich, flavorful sauce. With the oven mitts, carefully place the skillet in the middle of the oven and bake until the meat breaks apart easily with a fork, 1½ to 2 hours.

horseradish mashed potatoes

2 pounds russet or Yukon Gold potatoes, peeled and quartered

½ teaspoon salt, plus more for seasoning

6 tablespoons heavy cream or half-and-half

3 tablespoons unsalted butter

3 tablespoons mascarpone or sour cream

1 tablespoon creamy horseradish

Freshly ground black pepper

* Place the potatoes in a large stockpot with the ½ teaspoon salt and enough water to cover. Bring to a rapid boil over high heat. Reduce the heat to medium and cook until soft; drain. Return the potatoes to the pot and cook over medium heat for 3 to 5 minutes, allowing them to absorb some of the moisture. Reduce the heat to low, and shake the potatoes over the heat for 3 minutes. Mash with a potato ricer, using medium-wide holes.

* In a small saucepan over low heat, mix together the cream, butter, mascarpone, and horseradish. Cook for 5 minutes. Be careful not to let this mixture come to a boil.

* Slowly pour the cream mixture into the potatoes while whipping the potatoes with a fork or whisk. Mix until light and fluffy. Season to taste with salt and pepper and serve hot.

schultz sunday supper pot roast

In Missoula, Montana, Sunday dinner at our cousin's home is a family affair. The pot roast cooks slowly on top of the stove until it is fork-tender, and the onions have melted down to make a wonderful gravy. You need to use a deeper skillet, one with 4-inch sides, or a cast iron Dutch oven. The semi-dry roasting in this recipe develops the rich flavor of the meat. Serve the roast with carrots and fingerling potatoes.

MAKES 6 SERVINGS

1 tablespoon extra-virgin olive oil
1 (3½-pound) chuck roast
Salt and freshly ground black pepper
1 medium yellow onion, thinly sliced
1 cup boiling water

GRAVY
2 tablespoons all-purpose flour
½ cup water
Additional 1½ cups water, or ½ cup water and 1 cup heavy cream

❖ To prepare the pot roast, warm the olive oil in a 4-inch-deep 10- or 12-inch cast iron skillet over medium-high heat. Season the roast with salt and pepper, place in the skillet, and brown for 5 minutes on each side. Add the onions and boiling water. Cover with aluminum foil and bake at 325°F for 2½ to 3 hours, until fork-tender.

❖ To make gravy from the juices, transfer the meat to a platter and keep warm. In a small bowl, whisk together the flour and the ½ cup water until well blended. Stir the mixture into the juices in the pan. Cook over medium-low heat, stirring, until the sauce thickens. Gradually add the 1½ cups water (or for a delicious creamy gravy, add ½ cup water and 1 cup heavy cream), and continue to stir until smooth and thickened. Spoon over the sliced pot roast.

NOTE: Cold leftover pot roast, chopped with sweet yellow onions and mixed with a little horseradish and mayonnaise, makes a great sandwich spread.

open-face sloppy joes

When you want something quick to serve your family, Open-Face Sloppy Joes please all ages. The ground beef browns so well in the cast iron skillet. Serve with Crispy Slaw (recipe follows).

MAKES 4 SERVINGS

❋ Warm the oil and butter in a 10- or 12-inch cast iron skillet over medium heat. Add the chopped onions and cook, stirring occasionally, for 5 minutes. Add the bell pepper and ground beef, stirring to crumble and brown the meat. Add the tomato sauce, ketchup, and Worcestershire sauce and simmer for 15 minutes.

❋ Place a toasted bun, open face, buttered side up, on each plate, and spoon the meat mixture over the top.

1 tablespoon vegetable oil
1 tablespoon salted butter
1 cup chopped yellow onion (about ½ onion)
½ cup chopped red bell pepper (about ½ pepper)
12 ounces lean ground beef
2 cups tomato sauce
¼ cup ketchup
1 to 2 teaspoons Worcestershire sauce
4 small hamburger buns, toasted and buttered

crispy slaw

MAKES 4 TO 6 SERVINGS

❋ Place the cabbage in a large bowl. Cover with cold water and 8 to 10 ice cubes. Let crisp for 15 minutes. Make the dressing by mixing the vinegar, mayonnaise, and sugar together. Drain the cabbage in a colander. Transfer to a serving bowl, add the carrots and bell pepper, and gently toss with the dressing to coat. Sprinkle with salt and pepper to taste. Serve alongside the sloppy Joes or on top, with a toasted top bun.

½ head green cabbage, finely sliced
¼ cup white wine vinegar
3 tablespoons mayonnaise
1 tablespoon sugar
2 large carrots, peeled and grated
¼ red bell pepper, seeds and ribs removed and cut into thin strips
Salt and freshly ground black pepper

no-fail beef stew

The key to successful beef stew is to make the beef melt-in-your-mouth tender. You first need to brown it well, which a cast iron pan does perfectly. When the stew is simmering, you don't want to add excess moisture to it by allowing condensation to form on the lid. To prevent this, wrap the lid in a dish towel (the corners should be on top of the lid) before placing it tightly on the skillet. Serve this stew over mashed potatoes or polenta.

MAKES 6 TO 8 SERVINGS

2 pounds beef stew meat

½ teaspoon salt

¼ teaspoon freshly ground black pepper

4 to 5 tablespoons extra-virgin olive oil, divided

8 ounces white or cremini mushrooms, cleaned, stems trimmed, and quartered

1 yellow onion, diced

2 stalks celery, halved lengthwise and sliced ¼ inch thick

2 large carrots, peeled and cut diagonally into 2-inch-thick slices

2 cloves garlic, minced

1 teaspoon fresh thyme leaves, or ½ teaspoon dried thyme

2 (14.5-ounce) cans crushed tomatoes, with their juice (see note)

1 cup full-bodied red wine (such as cabernet sauvignon)

1½ cups water

2 bay leaves

1 tablespoon Worcestershire sauce

* Season the meat with the salt and pepper. Heat 1 tablespoon of the olive oil in a deep 12-inch cast iron skillet or Dutch oven over medium-high heat. Working in three or four batches, add the beef to the pan and cook, browning on all sides, for about 5 minutes. Transfer the browned beef to a plate, add another tablespoon of olive oil to the pan, and add the next batch of beef. You need to work quickly between batches so that the meat bits in the pan don't blacken. Repeat with the remaining batches.

* Reduce the heat to medium, and add 1 tablespoon olive oil to the pan. Add the mushrooms, onions, celery, carrots, garlic, and thyme. Cook, stirring occasionally, for 5 minutes. Return the beef to the pan, and stir in the tomatoes and their liquid, wine, water, and bay leaves. Bring to a light boil, and then reduce the heat to low. Cover (see the note at the beginning of the recipe) and simmer for 1 hour.

* Add the Worcestershire sauce and olives and cook, covered, for another 20 to 30 minutes. Remove the bay leaves.

* If the stew seems to have too much liquid and you would like to thicken it, place a large strainer over a large bowl and

pour the stew into the strainer to drain off the liquid. Move the strainer to another bowl and set aside. Pour the stew liquid back into the pan and bring to a boil over medium-high heat until it starts to thicken. Do not reduce for too long or the sauce will become too salty. Return the beef and vegetables to the pan, warm, and serve garnished with parsley.

¼ to ½ cup pitted or unpitted green olives

3 tablespoons fresh chopped parsley, for garnish

NOTE: We like Muir Glen fire-roasted crushed tomatoes. If you can't find them, add ½ teaspoon paprika to regular crushed tomatoes. You can substitute canned chopped tomatoes.

slow-roasted beef brisket

with Apple Cider–Ginger Barbecue Sauce and Caramelized Sweet Onions

This is comfort food at its best! Slow-simmered with a sweet-and-sour sauce that has a hint of ginger, the meat becomes very tender. Use any leftovers from this dish for Beef Brisket Hash with Yukon Gold Potatoes (page 26).

MAKES 4 TO 6 SERVINGS

APPLE CIDER–GINGER BARBECUE SAUCE
¾ cup packed light brown sugar
1 cup ketchup
½ cup apple cider vinegar
1 tablespoon Worcestershire sauce
¼ cup soy sauce
1 clove garlic, minced
1-inch piece fresh ginger, peeled and grated

CARAMELIZED ONIONS
2 tablespoons extra-virgin olive oil, plus more as needed
½ sweet yellow onion, cut into quarters and thinly sliced crosswise

1 (1- to 3-pound) beef brisket

❋ To prepare the barbecue sauce, place the brown sugar, ketchup, apple cider vinegar, Worcestershire sauce, soy sauce, garlic, and ginger in a medium saucepan. Simmer over medium-low heat for 10 minutes. Refrigerate until ready to use.

❋ Position a rack in the center of the oven and preheat to 300°F.

❋ To prepare the onions, spread the olive oil evenly in a 12-inch cast iron skillet over medium heat, add the onions, and cook, stirring occasionally, until golden. Remove from the pan and set aside.

❋ Turn up the heat to medium, add the brisket, and cook, turning once, until seared on both sides, about 5 minutes. You may need to add a bit more olive oil to keep the meat from sticking to the pan.

❋ Remove the skillet from the heat, and spread the barbecue sauce evenly over the top of the meat. Sprinkle the cooked onions over the brisket, cover the skillet tightly with foil, and bake until fork-tender, about 3 hours. To serve, cut crosswise into ½-inch slices.

seared pork chops

with Plum-Mustard-Cornichon Sauce

Known in Burgundy, France, as *côtes de porc vigneronnes* (grape growers' pork chops), this succulent and elegant dish is traditionally served after a day spent harvesting grapes. Susan Herrmann Loomis, a chef, teacher, and cookbook author who lives in France, inspired this recipe. It has the perfect balance of salty and sweet from the plums, capers, and cornichons.

MAKES 6 SERVINGS

* Position a rack in the center of the oven and preheat to 350°F.

* To prepare the sauce, melt the butter in a small saucepan over medium-low heat. Add the shallots, garlic, and water to the pan and cook for 2 minutes. Whisk in the capers, plum butter, cornichons, and mustard. Season to taste with salt and pepper. Set aside.

* To prepare the pork chops, melt 1 tablespoon of the butter with 1 tablespoon of the olive oil in a 10- or 12-inch cast iron skillet over medium heat. Season the pork chops with salt and pepper. Add 3 chops to the skillet and cook, turning once, until lightly browned, about 3 minutes on each side. Transfer to a plate and set aside. Repeat with the 3 remaining pork chops, adding 1 more tablespoon each of butter and olive oil to the skillet.

* When all of the pork chops are browned, place them in the skillet and transfer to the oven. (You may need to use 2 skillets to fit all 6 chops; add 1 tablespoon each of butter and olive oil to the second skillet before adding the pork.) Bake until a meat thermometer inserted into the center of the

(continued)

PLUM-MUSTARD-CORNICHON SAUCE
2 tablespoons salted butter
1 large shallot, minced (about 3 tablespoons)
1 large clove garlic, minced
½ cup water
1 tablespoon capers, mashed or lightly chopped
2 tablespoons plum butter (see note, page 74)
2 tablespoons minced cornichons (about 4 cornichons) (see note, page 74)
1 tablespoon Dijon mustard
Salt and freshly ground black pepper

2 tablespoons butter, divided
2 tablespoons extra-virgin olive oil, divided
6 (8- to 10-ounce) bone-in pork loin rib chops, ¾ inch thick
Salt and freshly ground black pepper

2 tablespoons chopped fresh parsley, for garnish

chops registers 150°F, about 8 minutes. (The pork will continue to cook after it is removed from the oven.) Transfer the pork chops to a warm serving platter and cover lightly with foil to keep warm. If the pork chops have released any juices onto the platter, add them to the sauce. Warm the sauce over low heat and whisk briefly, and then pour the warm sauce over the pork chops. Garnish with parsley and serve.

NOTE: Cornichons are tiny, brine-packed French pickles. They are available at most large or specialty grocery stores, where you can also find plum butter. To make your own plum butter, just place 6 to 8 pitted prunes in a blender together with 3 tablespoons hot water, and purée until smooth.

fennel-seared pork tenderloin

with Blackberry Sauce

This technique of pan-searing meat in the skillet and then finishing it in the oven keeps the meat moist and tender. The searing creates a crust, which seals in the juices. Make the sauce first and then cook the tenderloin. The sweetness of the onions and the tartness of the blackberries complement the savory flavor of the fennel-rubbed pork.

MAKES 4 SERVINGS

* Position a rack in the center of the oven and preheat to 350°F.

* To prepare the fennel salt, spread the fennel seed in a cast iron skillet and roast in the oven for 6 minutes. Grind in a spice grinder, and then mix with the sea salt in a small bowl.

* Increase the oven heat to 375°F.

* To prepare the blackberry sauce, melt the butter in a medium saucepan over medium heat. Add the onions and cook, stirring occasionally, for 5 minutes. Stir in the mustard. Add the chicken stock and cook, stirring, for several minutes. Add the blackberries and honey, reduce the heat to medium-low, and simmer until the sauce begins to thicken, about 10 minutes. Strain half of the sauce into a bowl, reserving the juices. Add these juices back to the remaining sauce in the pan. Discard the berries and onions left in the strainer.

* To prepare the pork, rub the tenderloin evenly with 1 tablespoon of the fennel salt. Heat a 10- or 12-inch cast

(continued)

FENNEL SALT
2 tablespoons fennel seed
4 teaspoons sea salt

BLACKBERRY SAUCE
2 tablespoons salted butter
½ medium yellow onion, thinly sliced and cut into 1-inch pieces
2 teaspoons Dijon mustard
1 cup chicken stock
2½ cups fresh or frozen blackberries
¼ cup honey

1 pork tenderloin, about 1 pound
2 tablespoons extra-virgin olive oil

iron skillet over medium-high heat. Add the olive oil, and let it heat for 1 minute. Add the tenderloin and cook until browned on all sides, about 6 minutes. Place the skillet in the oven and roast, uncovered, for 20 minutes. Remove from the oven and let rest for several minutes. Pour any excess juice from the cooked tenderloin into the blackberry sauce. Reheat the sauce quickly. Slice the tenderloin crosswise, arrange on a platter, and spoon the warm blackberry sauce over the top.

chicken paillards

with Red and Yellow Peppers and Kalamata Olives

The peppers, capers, olives, and lemons in this dish are colorful on the plate, and their flavors all blend together to form a delicious sauce for the chicken. Have everything ready ahead of time, and then quickly sauté and serve when it's time to eat.

MAKES 4 SERVINGS

* Preheat the oven to 250°F, and place a serving platter in the oven to warm.

* Place the chicken breasts, one at a time, in a large resealable plastic bag (slightly opened), and pound lightly with a mallet or rolling pin until flattened to ½ inch thick.

* Warm 2 tablespoons of the olive oil in a 10- or 12-inch cast iron skillet over medium heat. Add the pepper strips and cook, stirring occasionally, for 3 minutes. Transfer to a small plate and set aside.

* Mix the flour, salt, and pepper in a flat dish. Lightly coat the chicken breasts in the flour mixture, shaking off any excess flour. Warm the butter and remaining 1 tablespoon olive oil in the skillet over medium heat until the butter melts. Add the chicken breasts and cook until golden brown on one side, about 3 minutes. Turn and cook until golden brown on the other side, about 3 minutes longer.

* Transfer to a warm serving platter. Sprinkle the reserved peppers, olives, capers, and lemon juice over the chicken. Garnish with chopped parsley and serve.

4 boneless, skinless chicken breast halves (2 whole chicken breasts cut in half)
3 tablespoons extra-virgin olive oil, divided
1 medium red bell pepper, seeds and ribs removed, sliced into ½-inch strips
1 medium yellow bell pepper, seeds and ribs removed, sliced into ½-inch strips
¼ cup all-purpose flour
1 teaspoon salt
½ teaspoon freshly ground black pepper
1 tablespoon salted butter

⅓ cup kalamata olives, pitted
1 tablespoon capers, rinsed and drained
1 to 2 tablespoons fresh lemon juice
Chopped fresh parsley, for garnish

smoked pork chops

with Apples, Fresh Thyme, and Sweet Onions

A perfect fall dinner—savory and sweet. You can find smoked pork chops in specialty meat markets or most grocery stores. For the apples, we like to use the Honeycrisp, Granny Smith, or Fuji varieties. The smoky, salty flavor of the pork chops is complemented by the sweet apples. Serve with Rosemary Roasted Potatoes (page 123).

MAKES 4 SERVINGS

2 tablespoons extra-virgin olive oil, divided, plus more for grilling the pork chops
½ medium sweet yellow onion, very thinly sliced
3 apples, peeled, quartered, and cored
1 teaspoon fresh thyme leaves, or ½ teaspoon dried thyme
½ teaspoon salt
4 smoked pork chops, ½ inch thick
1 tablespoon packed light brown sugar
Freshly ground black pepper

* Heat 1 tablespoon of the oil in a 10- or 12-inch cast iron skillet. Add the onions and cook over medium heat for 5 minutes, stirring occasionally. Slice the apples crosswise into ½-inch-thick slices and add to the onions. Add the thyme and salt.

* Cover and simmer on top of the stove over medium-low heat for 10 minutes. Meanwhile, preheat the oven to 350°F.

* Rub the pork chops on both sides with the remaining tablespoon of olive oil and rub in the brown sugar on both sides. Season lightly with salt and pepper. Brush a cast iron grill pan generously with olive oil and heat over medium-high heat. Place the pork chops on the hot pan.

* Sear the chops for 2 minutes, turning them on a 45° angle to achieve crisscross grill marks, and then cook for 2 minutes more. Turn them over, brushing with a little more olive oil if needed, and repeat on the other side. Place the chops on the apple mixture, cover with aluminum foil, and bake for 10 minutes. Serve immediately.

skillet-roasted chicken

with Rosemary, Garlic, and Maple-Balsamic Glaze

We love the flavor and moistness of this chicken. The inside stays moist and the outside crispy and flavorful. Serve with braised greens or a green salad. Use leftovers for sandwiches or as a tasty pizza topping along with Mama Lil's Sweet Peppers (see Resources, page 189).

MAKES 4 TO 6 SERVINGS

2 tablespoons fresh rosemary (about 5 sprigs), plus 5 more whole rosemary sprigs

2 cloves garlic

Grated zest of 1 lemon (reserve ½ of the lemon to roast in the chicken)

¼ cup olive oil

¼ cup balsamic vinegar

¼ cup maple syrup

1 tablespoon lemon juice

1 (4-pound) whole chicken

2 pounds red potatoes, scrubbed and halved if small, or quartered if large

Salt and freshly ground black pepper

* Position a rack in the center of the oven and preheat to 400°F.

* Using a mortar and pestle, crush together the 2 tablespoons rosemary, garlic, and lemon zest until they form a paste. Place the paste in a bowl and whisk in the olive oil, balsamic vinegar, maple syrup, and lemon juice. (You can also use a blender for this step. Place the rosemary, garlic, lemon zest, vinegar, maple syrup, and lemon juice in a blender and blend until combined. With the blender running, drizzle in the olive oil.)

* Remove the neck and giblets from the chicken, and then rinse the chicken and pat dry. Rub the body and neck cavity with salt and pepper. Using your fingers, loosen the skin and rub the rosemary mixture under the skin over the breast, thighs, and drumsticks. Halve the lemon you used for zesting and place half in the cavity, along with the 5 whole rosemary sprigs.

* Place the potatoes in a 10- or 12-inch cast iron skillet. Season with salt and pepper, and then place the chicken, breast side up, on top of the potatoes. Roast in the oven for 55 to 65 minutes for a 4-pound bird. (Add 8 minutes for each additional pound.) After 20 minutes, baste the chicken

with the pan juices. Repeat 20 minutes later. Roast until a meat thermometer inserted in the thickest part of the thigh, without touching a bone, reads 170° to 175°F and the juices run clear. If you want the dark meat to be fork-tender, roast to 180°F.

* Remove the chicken from the pan, and place it on a sheet of foil to rest for 5 minutes. (You can return the potatoes to the oven and reduce the heat to 300°F to keep them warm.) Meanwhile, reduce the pan juices slightly. After carving the chicken, place it on warmed plates with the potatoes. Spoon some of the reduced pan juices over the top and serve.

tom's brick chicken

with Oven-Roasted Potatoes and Asparagus

Tom Kramis likes to fix chicken for his family this way. Ask your butcher to remove the backbone so that the chicken will lie flat, or follow the instructions in the note below to butterfly it yourself. Use a foil-wrapped brick or another, smaller cast iron skillet wrapped in foil and placed on top of the chicken to weigh it down while cooking. This flattens the chicken and crisps the skin. If you can, use free-range chicken, as it is more moist and tender.

MAKES 4 SERVINGS

* Preheat oven to 400°F.

* Rub the chicken all over with the 2 tablespoons of oil. Mix the rosemary, oregano, thyme, Italian herbs, and lemon zest in a small bowl, and then rub the mixture all over the chicken. Sprinkle the chicken with the sea salt and pepper.

* Warm the ¼ cup of oil in a 10- or 12-inch cast iron skillet over medium heat. Place the chicken in the skillet, skin side down. Weight down the chicken with a foil-wrapped brick or a second smaller skillet. Cook the chicken for 10 minutes.

* Meanwhile, in a medium bowl, toss the potatoes with 2 tablespoons of the oil, the herbs de Provence, and salt, and set aside.

* Turn the chicken over and cook, weighted down, for 5 minutes. Then turn it skin side down again, replace the brick, and distribute the potatoes around the chicken. Place the skillet in the oven and continue cooking for 15 minutes.

* Meanwhile, in the bowl that held the potatoes, toss the asparagus with the remaining tablespoon of oil, the lemon

(continued)

CHICKEN

1 (2½-pound) whole chicken, butterflied (see note, page 84)
¼ cup extra-virgin olive oil, plus 2 tablespoons for rubbing the chicken
1 teaspoon finely chopped fresh rosemary
1 teaspoon lightly chopped fresh oregano
1 teaspoon fresh thyme leaves
1 teaspoon dried Italian herbs or herbs de Provence
Zest of 1 lemon
1 teaspoon sea salt
Freshly ground black pepper

POTATOES AND ASPARAGUS

1 pound baby tri-color or red potatoes
3 tablespoons olive oil, divided
¼ teaspoon herbs de Provence
¼ teaspoon salt
1 bunch asparagus, trimmed and halved
1 teaspoon fresh lemon zest
Salt and freshly ground black pepper

zest, salt, and pepper. Remove the skillet from the oven, add the asparagus to the skillet in the same manner as the potatoes, and cook for 15 minutes longer, or until the chicken registers 160°F where the leg joins the breast on an instant-read thermometer.

* Carve the chicken into pieces and serve with the potatoes and asparagus.

NOTE: To butterfly a chicken, place the whole chicken on a cutting board, breast side down, legs pointing toward you. You can feel the backbone running down the center of the chicken. Using kitchen shears, cut to the right side of the breast bone (through the ribs) from the bottom of the chicken to the top, and then repeat on the left side, and remove the backbone. Using a pairing knife, make a slit through the cartilage that covers the breast-bone on the top part of the chicken. The breastbone will then be exposed (it is red). Run a pairing knife on both sides of the breastbone and remove the bone, wiggling out the bottom half. Flatten the chicken, trim off any excess fat, and remove any extra bones that stick out.

pork katsu

with Tonkatsu Sauce

This recipe is very popular all over Japan. You can use chicken instead of pork, the way they serve it in Hawaii. Kids love this dish with rice, daikon radish, and lightly dressed cabbage.

MAKES 4 SERVINGS

* In a small bowl, mix the mustard and hot water. In a small saucepan, combine the rest of the sauce ingredients and add the mustard water. Whisk over medium-low heat until small bubbles form. Reduce the heat to low, and cook the sauce for 4 to 5 minutes. Remove the pan from the heat and set aside.

* Preheat oven to 350°F.

* Rinse the pork, and pat it dry with paper towels. Trim the fat around the edges and make a few slits in the carved parts so that they do not curl up during cooking. Using a pestle or mallet, pound the pork until it has almost doubled in size or is half as thick as when you bought it.

* Heat the oil in a 10- or 12-inch cast iron skillet over medium heat until it registers 350°F on a deep-fat thermometer. Place the flour on a plate or in a shallow bowl. Pour the beaten eggs into a shallow dish. Place the panko in another shallow dish. Line a third plate with paper towels, and place it next to the skillet.

* Sprinkle the pork with salt and pepper. Place each pork chop in the flour, spooning flour over it to coat. Shake off any excess flour, and then dip each chop in the eggs, turning once to coat. Allow excess egg to drip off, and then roll each

(continued)

TONKATSU SAUCE

1 teaspoon dry mustard
2 teaspoons hot water
1 cup ketchup
3 tablespoons Worcestershire sauce
1 tablespoon soy sauce
1 tablespoon A.1. steak sauce (optional)
⅛ teaspoon ground allspice

KATSU

4 boneless pork chops or chicken breast halves
1 cup vegetable or peanut oil
1 cup all-purpose flour or potato starch
3 large eggs, beaten with 1 teaspoon vegetable oil
1 cup panko bread crumbs
Salt and freshly ground black pepper

Cooked rice, for serving
1 lemon, cut into wedges, for garnish
Thinly sliced or julienned daikon radish, for garnish
Sliced cabbage, for garnish

chop in the panko, pressing the crumbs to adhere. Set the chops on a plate.

* Carefully add 2 chops at a time to the hot oil. Fry on one side until golden brown, about 3 minutes. Using a fork or tongs, carefully flip the chops over and repeat on the other side. Remove with tongs or a slotted spoon to the paper towel–lined plate. Repeat with the remaining 2 chops.

* Put the chops on a baking sheet and bake for 10 minutes, or until they are firm to the touch, release clear liquid when pierced with a knife, or register 160°F on an instant-read thermometer. Remove the chops from the oven and allow them to rest for 5 minutes. Meanwhile, reheat the sauce.

* To serve, cut the chops into 1-inch-thick slices and place a half to a whole chop (depending on appetite) on top of the rice. Ladle ¼ cup sauce over the top. Garnish with the lemon wedges, daikon, and cabbage.

pan-seared chicken

with Sausage, Fingerling Potatoes, and Green Beans

Serve this one-dish meal right in the skillet. The flavors complement each other and create delicious juices to spoon over the top of each serving.

MAKES 4 SERVINGS

* Boil the potatoes in a stockpot until tender. Drain and let cool. Cut in half lengthwise and set aside.

* Pour an inch of water into a shallow pan and bring to a boil. Add the green beans. Cover and cook just until they start to soften, 3 to 5 minutes. Drain the beans and spread out onto paper towels to cool.

* Warm a 10- or 12-inch cast iron skillet over medium-high heat. Add 2 tablespoons of the olive oil. Season the chicken breasts with salt and pepper and cook for 4 minutes on each side. Transfer to a platter and reserve.

* Add the remaining 2 tablespoons olive oil to the skillet, and reduce the heat to medium. Add the onions and garlic to the pan and cook, stirring occasionally, until soft. Add the sausage to the skillet and cook for several minutes. Add the cooked potatoes and green beans. Mix together with a spatula. Cut each chicken breast in half crosswise and place on top of the potatoes and beans. Sprinkle the bell pepper strips over the top. Add the chicken stock. Cover loosely with aluminum foil, reduce the heat to medium-low, and cook for about 15 minutes. Serve from the skillet.

1 pound fingerling potatoes

8 ounces small green beans, stem ends removed

4 tablespoons extra-virgin olive oil, divided

4 bone-in chicken breasts, skin removed

Salt and freshly ground black pepper

1 cup finely chopped yellow onion

1 clove garlic, minced

12 ounces smoked andouille sausage, cut into ¼-inch-thick slices

½ red bell pepper, seeds and ribs removed and cut into thin strips

½ cup chicken stock

chicken with herbed dumplings

This recipe is a family favorite for a wintertime Sunday dinner, served with a fresh green salad. The herbs in the moist dumplings and the coarse salt on top really set this dish apart. The dumplings usually disappear first, but we like to serve the leftover chicken and vegetables over mashed potatoes the next day.

MAKES 6 TO 8 SERVINGS

2 pounds boneless, skinless chicken breast halves

Salt and freshly ground black pepper

3 tablespoons olive oil, divided

3 tablespoons unsalted butter

1 yellow onion, peeled and diced

4 ounces small white mushrooms, cleaned, stems trimmed, and halved

¼ cup all-purpose flour

3 cups chicken stock

¾ cup heavy cream

3 tablespoons dry sherry

4 medium carrots, peeled and cut into ½-inch slices

2 celery stalks, cut into ½-inch pieces

1 bay leaf

¼ teaspoon ground or freshly grated nutmeg

1 teaspoon finely chopped fresh oregano leaves

1 teaspoon finely chopped fresh thyme leaves

¾ cup fresh or frozen peas (optional)

* Position a rack in the center of the oven and preheat to 425°F.

* To prepare the chicken, rinse the chicken breasts, pat them dry, and cut them into 1-inch strips. Season with salt and pepper and divide into three batches. Heat 1 tablespoon of the olive oil in a 10- or 12-inch cast iron skillet over medium-high heat. Add the first batch of chicken and cook, turning once, until browned on both sides, about 5 minutes. Transfer to a cutting board and repeat with the remaining two batches, adding another tablespoon of olive oil for each batch. Set the chicken aside.

* In the same skillet, melt the butter over medium heat. Add the onion and mushrooms and cook, stirring occasionally, until the onions have softened, about 5 minutes. Stir in the flour. Slowly add the chicken stock, cream, and sherry, whisking often, and bring to a boil over medium heat. Reduce the heat and add the carrots, celery, bay leaf, nutmeg, oregano, and thyme. Generously season to taste with salt and pepper and simmer for 5 minutes. Return the chicken strips to the skillet and cook over medium heat for 5 minutes. Mix in the peas.

* To prepare the dumplings, whisk together the flour, cornmeal, baking powder, and salt in a large bowl. Cut the chilled butter into tablespoon-sized slices. Using a pastry blender and working quickly so that the butter remains cold, cut in the butter until the pieces are pea-sized. (You can also transfer the flour mixture to a food processor fitted with a steel blade, add the butter, and pulse 5 or 6 times.) Gently mix in the rosemary, using your hands or a spatula. Add the milk and mix gently just until the ingredients are wet and slightly sticky.

* Using a large spoon, scoop up some of the dumpling mixture and drop it on top of the chicken mixture. Repeat until all of the dumpling mixture is used (you should have about 10 dumplings). Sprinkle the tops with the kosher salt, and return the skillet to the oven. Bake until the dumplings are golden brown, 20 to 25 minutes. If you want to brown the tops of the dumplings more, brush the tops with melted butter and turn on the broiler for the last few minutes, keeping a close eye on the dumplings at this point. Serve from the skillet.

HERBED DUMPLINGS

1¼ cups all-purpose flour
⅔ cup cornmeal
2½ teaspoons baking powder
½ teaspoon salt
7 tablespoons chilled butter
3 teaspoons chopped fresh
   rosemary
⅔ cup whole milk
½ teaspoon kosher salt or fleur
   de sel

cornish game hens

with Preserved Lemons and Olives

Our friend Meriem Atowani Kass brought this recipe with her when she moved to Seattle from Casablanca. The olives and preserved lemons, a combination commonly used in Moroccan cooking, are a delicious addition to game hens. In Morocco, this dish is presented surrounded by many small dishes, such as Eggplant-Pepper Tapenade (page 52) and fresh tomato salsa. You can also serve this dish on top of a bed of couscous. Buy preserved lemons at a specialty grocery store, or see the recipe on page 93 to prepare your own. Note: You can use fresh lemons instead.

MAKES 2 TO 4 SERVINGS

* Position a rack in the center of the oven and preheat to 350°F.

* In a large bowl, mix together the onion, cilantro, garlic, ginger, saffron, 1 teaspoon of the paprika, olive oil, and lemon juice. Working in batches, place the hen pieces in the bowl with the sauce and toss to coat. Rub the pieces with the remaining tablespoon of paprika, sprinkle with salt and pepper, and place on a dish. Cover and marinate for 1 hour.

* Heat a 10- or 12-inch cast iron skillet over medium-high heat. Add 3 to 4 pieces of game hen at a time. Do not crowd the pan! Brown for 3 to 5 minutes on each side. Remove to a plate and continue in the same manner with the rest of the game hen. Return all pieces to the skillet, and pour the onion mixture over the hens, coating them well. Carefully pour in the water. Place the skillet over medium heat for 10 minutes. Transfer the skillet to the oven and bake, uncovered, for another 35 minutes.

(continued)

1 yellow onion, coarsely chopped

¼ cup chopped fresh cilantro, or 2 teaspoons ground coriander

2 cloves garlic, minced

2 teaspoons ground ginger

½ teaspoon saffron

1 tablespoon plus 1 teaspoon paprika

¼ cup olive oil

Juice of 2 lemons

2 Cornish game hens, cut in half and backbone removed (see note, page 84), or substitute 2 chicken breasts, 2 thighs, and 2 legs

Salt and freshly ground black pepper

1 cup water

1 cup green Greek olives (about 20 olives), pitted or unpitted

Peel of ½ preserved lemon, cut into ½-inch-thick slices

3 tablespoons chopped fresh cilantro, for garnish

* Meanwhile, place the olives and preserved lemon peel in a separate small saucepan. Add ¼ cup of the game hen sauce from the skillet. Bring the sauce to a boil, and warm the olives all the way through.

* Remove the skillet from the oven, and transfer the game hen pieces to a plate. Set aside. Place the skillet over medium-high heat, and bring the sauce to a boil until it begins to thicken, about 5 minutes.

* To serve, pour the sauce from the skillet over the game hen. Garnish with the olives and lemon peel and any of the sauce that remains. Sprinkle with the cilantro and serve.

preserved lemons

We love to have a jar of preserved lemons standing by. They are a salty yet sweet, very fragrant addition to lamb or fish. They are surprisingly simple to prepare and also make a lovely gift. You can add whole cloves or whole allspice to the jar to give these golden gems a different flavor. Slice the rind thinly and use in salads and with cheeses. Use the flesh (seeds removed) in stews and sauces.

5 ripe lemons
⅓ cup kosher salt
Sterilized quart jar
1 bay leaf
1 star anise (optional)
4 to 5 black peppercorns
Juice of 2 lemons

✻ Quarter the lemons lengthwise, cutting only up to the bottom inch, so you can fan the lemons open. Sprinkle the inside of each open lemon with 2 teaspoons of the salt, and then close the wedges back up. Add 2 of the lemons to the jar, along with the bay leaf, star anise, and peppercorns. Sprinkle with 2 teaspoons salt and add the lemon juice. Add the remaining 3 lemons and another 2 teaspoons salt to the jar. Screw the lid on tightly, and let the jar sit in a dark place for 1 month, until the lemons become soft and turn a mustard color. Open the jar each week and press down on the lemons to release more juices. Shake the jar occasionally. Rinse the lemons before using. For storage, add olive oil, cover, and refrigerate. They will last for months.

grandpa don's picnic fried chicken

Grandpa loved to picnic. At any outdoor event, he would bring his cooler filled with fried chicken, potato salad, and watermelon. While his potato salad (recipe follows) isn't a skillet recipe, we always serve the two together.

MAKES 6 SERVINGS

3½ pounds chicken pieces, skin removed (cut the breast pieces in half crosswise)
1 tablespoon salt, plus more for seasoning
2 teaspoons freshly ground black pepper, plus more for seasoning
2 cups all-purpose flour
Canola oil, for frying

✤ Wash the chicken and dry thoroughly with paper towels. Season lightly with salt and pepper. Place the flour, 1 tablespoon salt, and 2 teaspoons pepper in a medium-sized paper bag. Shake to mix. Add half of the chicken pieces, close the bag tightly, and shake gently to coat the chicken. Transfer the chicken to a rack and repeat with the remaining chicken.

✤ Pour the oil into a 12-inch cast iron skillet to a depth of ¼ inch, or use a deep 10-inch skillet and pour the oil to a depth of 3 inches. Heat over medium heat. Carefully place 4 to 5 chicken pieces into the warm oil, standing back in case it spatters. (We like to use a spatter guard, available at cookware shops. See Resources, page 189.) Don't crowd the pan. Cook until the chicken is golden brown on one side. Turn and brown the other side. Repeat with the remaining chicken pieces. Remove the skillet from the burner, and pour off the excess oil from the pan. Lower the heat to medium-low. Return the skillet to the heat, add all of the chicken, and cover, leaving the lid partially ajar to prevent excess steaming. Cook for 40 minutes more. Remove the chicken from the pan and serve, or cool in the refrigerator and then pack into a plastic container with a tight-fitting lid and place in a cooler with ice packs.

grandpa don's potato salad

MAKES 6 SERVINGS

2 pounds Yukon Gold potatoes, well scrubbed and cut into quarters

½ sweet onion, thinly sliced and then chopped

4 hard-boiled eggs, peeled

1 cup mayonnaise, plus more as needed

1 teaspoon Colman's dry mustard

Salt and freshly ground black pepper

❋ Place the potatoes in a deep stockpot, cover with water, and boil until tender. Drain and let cool to room temperature. Peel the potatoes and cut into bite-size pieces. Place in a medium bowl. Sprinkle the chopped onions over the top, cover with plastic wrap, and refrigerate until well chilled.

❋ When ready to serve, cut up the eggs and add to the potatoes. Add the mayonnaise and mustard and mix well. Add more mayonnaise if you want a creamier consistency. Season to taste with salt and pepper.

chicken with calvados and cream

Calvados is a wonderful apple brandy that is made in the Pays d'Auge region of Normandy, France. The brand most commonly found in the United States is Grand Solage Boulard, which is made with up to 120 varieties of apples. We always have a bottle on hand to flavor sauces for pork, duck, and mussels or to mix into homemade ice cream. Serve this dish with Roasted Carrots and Fennel with Fresh Dill (page 141).

MAKES 4 TO 6 SERVINGS

3 tablespoons extra-virgin olive oil, divided

3 tablespoons butter, divided

3 yellow onions, cut into ¼-inch-thick slices

1 (3½- to 4-pound) whole chicken, separated into 2 breasts, 2 thighs, 2 wings, and 2 legs

Sea salt and freshly ground black pepper

2 apples (Jonagold or Gala), peeled, cored, and cut into 2-inch-thick slices

¼ cup Calvados

¼ cup heavy cream

½ cup chicken stock

6 fresh thyme sprigs

1 bay leaf

2 tablespoons chopped fresh flat-leaf parsley, for garnish

✢ Position a rack in the center of the oven and preheat to 400°F.

✢ Heat 1 tablespoon olive oil and 1 tablespoon butter in a 10- or 12-inch cast iron skillet over medium heat. Add the onions and cook, stirring occasionally, for 10 minutes, until softened but not browned. Transfer to a plate and set aside.

✢ Increase the heat to medium-high. In the same skillet, heat 1 tablespoon of the olive oil. Season the chicken with sea salt and pepper. Add half of the chicken pieces to the skillet and cook, turning occasionally, until golden brown on all sides. Transfer to a plate. Repeat with the second batch of chicken, adding the remaining tablespoon of olive oil. Set the chicken aside.

✢ Reduce the heat to medium. Add the remaining 2 tablespoons butter to the skillet. Add the apples and cook, stirring occasionally, until lightly golden and just slightly soft, about 5 minutes. Stir in the Calvados, cream, chicken stock, and thyme sprigs. Return the onions and chicken to the pan, mixing gently. Add the bay leaf.

✴ Place the skillet in the oven and bake for 20 minutes. Turn over all the chicken pieces and cook until the chicken is a deep golden brown and the juices run clear, about 20 minutes longer. Remove from the oven and sprinkle with parsley, salt, and pepper. Serve hot.

pan-seared duck breasts

with Orange-Thyme Sauce

Leaving the skin on the duck breast gives the duck its wonderful flavor, along with a delicious, crispy skin. If you don't have time to make the rub, you can just salt and pepper the skin because the sauce is so flavorful. You can also double or triple the spice rub and keep it on hand for your next duck, chicken, or pork dinner. Duck breasts are available in the frozen section of specialty grocery stores.

MAKES 4 SERVINGS

SPICE RUB

2 teaspoons kosher salt or fleur de sel
1 tablespoon packed light brown sugar
2 teaspoons fennel seed
1 tablespoon fresh rosemary
2 teaspoons coriander seed, or 1 teaspoon ground coriander
½ teaspoon ground ginger
1 teaspoon fresh oregano
2 large sage leaves
1 teaspoon fresh thyme leaves
½ teaspoon grated lemon zest

4 boneless, skin-on duck breasts (about 2 pounds total), at room temperature

ORANGE-THYME SAUCE

¼ cup dry sherry
¼ cup sherry vinegar
2 tablespoons orange juice
½ cup low-sodium chicken stock
2 teaspoons honey
1 teaspoon coarsely chopped thyme leaves
1 tablespoon unsalted butter

❋ To prepare the rub, combine the salt, brown sugar, fennel seed, rosemary, coriander seed, ginger, oregano, sage, thyme, and lemon zest in a coffee or spice grinder and grind until smooth. You can use a mortar and pestle if you don't have an electric grinder.

❋ Position a rack in the center of the oven and preheat to 425°F.

❋ To prepare the duck, rinse the breasts and pat dry. Trim any extra skin from the meat side of the breasts, leaving a ¼-inch overhang on the edges. Pull the tendon out of the breast, and pat the tender back into place. With a sharp knife, score the skin in a crosshatch pattern, making 6 to 8 cuts, ½ inch deep, in one direction and another 6 to 8 cuts in the other direction. Try not to cut through the meat. Coat both sides of the duck breasts with the spice rub mixture.

❋ Heat a 10- or 12-inch cast iron skillet over medium-high heat for 3 minutes. Add the duck breasts to the skillet, skin side down, and sear for 5 minutes. The skin should be crisp and golden brown.

❋ Reduce the heat to medium-low, turn the breasts over and cook for 2 minutes, and then place the skillet in the oven.

Roast until the duck is cooked to your liking—6 to 7 minutes for medium-rare (135°F on a meat thermometer). Cook a few minutes longer for medium. (Make sure not to cook the duck for too long, or it will toughen.) Transfer the duck to a plate and cover with aluminum foil to keep warm.

❋ To prepare the sauce, discard all but 2 tablespoons fat from the skillet, and place the skillet over medium-high heat. Add the sherry, sherry vinegar, and orange juice, scraping up the browned bits and stirring them into the sauce. Boil until slightly reduced. Add the chicken stock, honey, and thyme and bring to a gentle boil until slightly reduced again, about 2 minutes. Reduce the heat to low and whisk in the butter.

❋ Slice the duck breasts ¼ inch thick at a 45° angle. Serve on warm plates, and spoon about 3 tablespoons of sauce over each serving.

quick-to-fix roasted chicken hash

After a long day at work, nothing is easier than picking up a freshly roasted chicken at the grocery store to make this simple, flavorful chicken hash for dinner. Serve with a green salad and crusty bread. No other pan will brown a hash like a cast iron pan. Use the leftover chicken to make soup for lunch the next day.

MAKES 4 SERVINGS

¼ cup (½ stick) salted butter

1½ cups chopped sweet yellow onion

6 cups peeled, diced (½-inch cubes), and cooked Yukon Gold potatoes (about 2 pounds)

4 cups roast chicken, cut into small pieces

¾ cup heavy cream, divided

Salt and freshly ground black pepper

1 teaspoon chopped fresh thyme

¼ cup chopped fresh parsley, for garnish

❋ Melt the butter in a 10-inch cast iron skillet over medium heat. Add the onions and cook, stirring occasionally, for 5 minutes. Add the potatoes. Stir and continue to cook for 5 minutes. Add the chicken, mix well, and continue to cook for several minutes more. Pour ½ cup of the cream over the top of the chicken mixture. Season to taste with salt, pepper, and thyme. Cook until nice and hot, 3 to 5 minutes longer. Pour the remaining ¼ cup cream over the top. Sprinkle with the parsley, season again with salt and pepper, and serve.

mussels, prawns, and halibut in coconut curry sauce

This recipe was adapted from our friend Jack, who owns Bai Pai Restaurant in Seattle. We love the way the seafood takes on the wonderful flavors of the sauce in this recipe. The mussels are perfectly plump, the prawns crisp, and the fish firm. There is enough extra sauce to pour over your rice.

MAKES 4 TO 6 SERVINGS

* Skim ¼ cup of the thick cream from the top of the coconut milk and set aside. Stir the remaining cream in with the rest of the coconut milk.

* Warm the oil and reserved coconut cream in a 10- or 12-inch cast iron skillet over medium heat until simmering. Add the curry paste, increase the heat to medium-high, and stir-fry until the oil separates and the paste is lightly browned. Lower the heat to medium and stir in the fish sauce, brown sugar, and salt. Add the coconut milk, lemongrass, and kaffir lime leaves. Bring to a boil, stirring occasionally.

* Add the mussels and prawns and cook for 3 to 4 minutes. Then add the halibut and continue cooking until the mussels open, the prawns turn pink, and the halibut is white throughout, 4 to 5 minutes more.

* Remove the lemongrass and kaffir lime leaves. Scatter the cilantro and basil over the top. Serve in individual bowls over the jasmine rice, with the lime wedges on the side.

NOTE: If you cannot find fresh kaffir lime leaves, you can substitute 2 teaspoons fresh lime juice.

2 cups canned coconut milk

¼ cup vegetable oil

1 to 2 tablespoons red curry paste (adjust to your heat preference)

1½ tablespoons fish sauce

1 teaspoon packed dark brown sugar

½ teaspoon salt

1 stalk lemongrass, white part only, cut in half lengthwise

4 fresh kaffir lime leaves (see note)

1 pound fresh mussels, scrubbed and debearded

8 ounces fresh or frozen tiger prawns, peeled and deveined

1½ pounds fresh halibut fillets, skin removed, cut in half lengthwise, and then into thirds

Leaves from 10 sprigs fresh cilantro

10 fresh Thai basil or other basil leaves, stems removed and coarsely chopped

Cooked jasmine rice, for serving

1 lime, cut into 6 to 8 wedges, for garnish

pan-seared wild king salmon

with Dill Tartar Sauce

In the Pacific Northwest, we are fortunate to be able to get wild king salmon year-round, either fresh or expertly frozen at sea. Here is an easy way to cook it indoors for a fast dinner. Simply sear the salmon in the skillet and finish cooking it in the oven.

MAKES 4 SERVINGS

DILL TARTAR SAUCE
½ cup mayonnaise
⅓ cup finely diced dill pickle
⅓ cup finely diced red onion
1 tablespoon fresh lemon juice
1 teaspoon fresh dill, finely
   chopped

SALMON RUB
½ teaspoon sea salt
¼ teaspoon freshly ground
   black pepper
¼ cup packed light brown sugar
2 teaspoons lemon zest
⅛ teaspoon paprika

4 (6-ounce) wild salmon fillets, 1
   inch thick, skin removed
2 tablespoons extra-virgin
   olive oil

* To prepare the sauce, in a small bowl mix together the mayonnaise, pickle, onion, lemon juice, and dill. Cover and chill.

* Position a rack in the center of the oven and preheat to 400°F.

* For the rub, combine the sea salt, pepper, brown sugar, lemon zest, and paprika. Sprinkle the rub over the top side of the salmon, and then gently pat with your fingers to distribute evenly. Warm the olive oil in a 10- or 12-inch cast iron skillet over medium-high heat. Place the salmon fillets in the skillet and cook for 2 minutes. Carefully turn over and cook for 2 minutes on the other side.

* Transfer the skillet to the oven and bake until the fish flakes easily when tested with a fork, about 6 minutes. Serve with the sauce.

baked halibut

with Fresh Fennel and Cucumber-Fennel Raita

The best halibut is available March through November. Firm and moist, it lends itself well to baking. Here, it is complemented nicely by the fresh cucumber sauce. Since asparagus season also begins in March, asparagus makes an excellent springtime accompaniment.

MAKES 4 SERVINGS

❋ To prepare the raita, mix together the sour cream, cucumber, fennel, mint, salt, and pepper in a medium bowl and refrigerate until ready to serve.

❋ To prepare the fish, position a rack in the center of the oven and preheat to 375°F.

❋ Place the sliced fennel in a 10- or 12-inch cast iron skillet. Lay the halibut fillets on top of the fennel and drizzle with the olive oil. Scatter the lemon slices, thyme, and sea salt over the top. Cover with foil and bake until the fish flakes easily when tested with a fork, 15 to 20 minutes. Season with salt and pepper to taste. Serve with the Cucumber-Fennel Raita.

CUCUMBER-FENNEL
RAITA
1 cup sour cream
½ cup diced cucumber (¼-inch
   pieces)
½ cup diced fennel bulb (¼-inch
   pieces)
1 teaspoon chopped fresh mint
   leaves
¼ teaspoon salt
¼ teaspoon coarsely ground
   black pepper

1 fresh fennel bulb, thinly sliced
4 (6- to 8-ounce) halibut fillets,
   1 inch thick, skin removed
½ cup extra-virgin olive oil
1 lemon, thinly sliced
1 tablespoon finely chopped
   fresh thyme leaves
1 teaspoon sea salt
Salt and freshly ground black
   pepper

pan-seared sea scallops

with Apple-Thyme Sauce and Bacon Crumbs

We love to sear scallops in a hot cast iron skillet—they turn golden brown and succulent. The sweetness of the apple cider with the ginger and thyme complements the scallops' sweet flavor. Serve these scallops with a simple watercress and roasted beet salad with a light citrus dressing.

MAKES 4 SERVINGS

APPLE-THYME SAUCE
⅓ cup apple cider
⅔ cup chicken stock
3 sprigs fresh thyme
3 tablespoons white wine
1 teaspoon Pernod (optional)
¼-inch slice fresh ginger, peeled and cut in half
5 tablespoons chilled butter

2 tablespoons extra-virgin olive oil, divided
2 tablespoons butter, divided
16 large sea scallops

3 strips bacon, cooked and crumbled or cut into ¼-inch pieces, for garnish
4 small sprigs fresh thyme or parsley, for garnish

✤ Preheat the oven to 250°F, and place 4 small, flat bowls or salad plates in the oven to warm.

✤ To prepare the sauce, place the cider, chicken stock, thyme sprigs, wine, Pernod, and ginger in a small saucepan over medium heat. Bring to a boil and cook until reduced slightly. Remove the thyme and the ginger slices. Remove the pan from the heat and set aside. (Adding the butter after cooking the scallops ensures that the sauce will not break when reheating.)

✤ To prepare the scallops, pat them dry with paper towels. Warm 1 tablespoon each of the olive oil and butter in a 10- or 12-inch cast iron skillet over medium heat for 2 minutes. Add 8 scallops to the pan and brown for 2 to 3 minutes on each side (they should release from the pan on their own). Transfer the scallops to a plate and cover with foil. Warm the remaining olive oil and butter in the skillet and sear the remaining scallops. Transfer to the plate.

✤ Return the saucepan to medium-low heat. Once the sauce is simmering slightly, reduce the heat to low and whisk in 1 tablespoon of the cold butter. When it is incorporated, whisk in another tablespoon. Turn off the heat and whisk in the remaining butter, 1 tablespoon at a time.

✤ Place 4 scallops in each warmed bowl and then ladle about ¼ cup of sauce over them. Sprinkle 1 tablespoon crumbled bacon over the top, and garnish with a thyme sprig. Serve immediately.

dungeness crab cakes
with Tarragon Aïoli

Crunchy on the outside, smooth and creamy on the inside, these crab cakes are a delicious way to use fresh Dungeness crabmeat for a simple but elegant dinner. The sweet flavor of the crab is complemented by the tangy aïoli. The crab cakes need to chill for at least 2 hours before cooking, so you'll want to plan ahead. Serve with your favorite coleslaw.

MAKES 12 CRAB CAKES

TARRAGON AÏOLI
1 egg
¼ teaspoon Colman's dry mustard
2 tablespoons fresh lemon juice
1 tablespoon fresh tarragon leaves (about 3 sprigs)
1 cup light olive oil
Salt and freshly ground black pepper

CRAB CAKES
¼ cup (½ stick) salted butter
½ cup finely diced yellow onion (about ½ onion)
¼ cup finely chopped red bell pepper (about ½ pepper)
2 teaspoons Dijon mustard
¼ cup chopped fresh parsley
½ cup mayonnaise
1 pound Dungeness crabmeat
1 tablespoon fresh lemon juice
¼ teaspoon Tabasco sauce
½ teaspoon Worcestershire sauce

✤ To prepare the aïoli, put the egg, dry mustard, lemon juice, and tarragon in a food processor or a blender and process briefly. Then, with the machine running on low speed, add the oil in a slow, steady stream until the mixture thickens. Season to taste with salt and pepper. Cover with plastic wrap and refrigerate until ready to serve.

✤ To prepare the crab cakes, melt the butter in a 10- or 12-inch cast iron skillet over low heat. Add the onion and bell pepper and cook for 5 minutes. Remove from the heat and let cool. Transfer to a glass bowl. Stir in the mustard, parsley, and mayonnaise. Add the crabmeat, lemon juice, Tabasco sauce, Worcestershire sauce, and soft bread crumbs and mix gently to combine. Refrigerate the mixture for at least 2 hours.

✤ After chilling, shape the crab mixture into 12 small, round cakes, 3 inches in diameter and ¾ inch thick. Place the panko crumbs in a shallow dish and press each cake into the crumbs, coating completely on both sides.

✳ In the same skillet over medium heat, heat enough butter and oil to coat the bottom of the pan. Fry the crab cakes in batches until golden brown, 2 to 3 minutes on each side. If necessary, place the finished crab cakes on a paper towel–lined baking sheet and keep warm in a 250°F oven until ready to serve. Serve with the aïoli.

½ cup soft bread crumbs
2 cups panko bread crumbs, or other coarse bread crumbs
Butter and vegetable oil, for frying

garlic roasted dungeness crab

We like our crab chilled and plain in the Northwest. Big bowls of cracked Dungeness crab are as good as it gets. But for special occasions we sometimes dress it up this way because the crab flavor still shines through.

MAKES 2 SERVINGS

¼ cup extra-virgin olive oil

4 cloves garlic, finely chopped

¼ cup finely minced fresh parsley

1 teaspoon sea salt

1 Dungeness crab, cooked, cleaned, and broken into pieces

Melted butter, for dipping

✢ Position a rack in the center of the oven and preheat to 400°F.

✢ Pour the olive oil into a 10- or 12-inch cast iron skillet. Add the garlic, parsley, and sea salt. Stir over medium heat for 3 minutes. Add the crab and stir to coat evenly with the garlic mixture. Place the skillet in the oven and bake for 10 minutes. Serve with warm melted butter for dipping and plenty of napkins!

pan-seared trout

with Almonds and Gremolata

Good trout is available year-round. The traditional French preparation, which combines the nutty flavors of the almonds and browned butter with the fresh trout, is our favorite. Serve with oven-roasted fingerling potatoes.

MAKES 4 SERVINGS

* Position a rack in the center of the oven and preheat to 250°F.

* Soak the trout fillets in the milk for 30 minutes. Strain the fillets, discarding the milk.

* Season the fillets with salt and pepper. Place the flour in a flat dish and dredge the fillets in the flour.

* Melt the butter in a 10- or 12-inch cast iron skillet over medium-low heat. Add the fillets and cook for 4 minutes on each side. Transfer to a platter and keep warm in the oven.

* Place the almonds in a separate small sauté pan over medium-low heat. Cook, stirring occasionally, until light brown, about 3 minutes.

* To prepare the gremolata, add the parsley, lemon zest, and garlic to a small bowl and mix well to combine.

* Sprinkle the almonds over the top of the trout fillets, top with gremolata, and serve immediately.

4 trout fillets
1 cup milk
Salt and freshly ground black
    pepper
¼ cup all-purpose flour
6 tablespoons salted butter
¼ cup sliced almonds

GREMOLATA
2 tablespoons chopped flat-leaf
    parsley
1 teaspoon lemon zest
1 clove garlic, minced

shellfish paella

This classic dish from Spain provides the perfect background for Northwest shellfish. The saffron gives it a beautiful golden color. You can add chicken, andouille sausage, and other shellfish, along with beans or artichoke hearts. There are so many variations, but this recipe is our favorite. When fresh Dungeness crab is in season, we like to serve the cooked crab legs and body meat on the side or on top of the finished paella. Note: At no point should you stir the paella after it goes in the oven or it will get mushy.

MAKES 6 SERVINGS

SOFRITO

¼ cup olive oil

½ cup diced onion

2 cloves garlic, minced

1 medium red bell pepper, seeds and ribs removed and cut into ¼-inch-wide, 1½-inch-long strips

1 large tomato, peeled, seeded, and finely chopped, or 1 cup fire-roasted Muir Glen tomatoes (see note, page 71), drained

PAELLA

1 tablespoon olive oil

½ pound firm precooked chorizo or other good smoky-hot sausage, cut into 1-inch-thick pieces

6 cups chicken broth or water

3 cups paella rice

1 teaspoon salt

¼ teaspoon saffron threads, ground or smashed with a pestle

½ teaspoon smoked paprika (see note)

* To prepare the sofrito, warm the oil in a 12-inch cast iron skillet over medium-high heat. When the oil is hot, add the onion, garlic, bell pepper, and tomato. Cook, stirring often, for 5 minutes, and then reduce the heat to medium and continue to cook until a thick paste starts to form, about 15 minutes. Remove the sofrito to a bowl and set aside.

* Preheat the oven to 400°F.

* To prepare the paella, warm the olive oil in a 12- or 14-inch cast iron skillet over medium heat. When the oil is hot, add the chorizo and brown it for about 2 minutes on each side. Remove to a plate and set aside.

* In a large saucepan, add the chicken broth and bring it to a boil. Turn off the heat.

* Add the sofrito, rice, salt, saffron, and paprika to the skillet and stir to mix. Pour in the hot chicken broth, stirring constantly, and bring it back to a boil over high heat. When the broth is boiling, remove the skillet quickly from the heat and add the mussels, clams, and prawns, tucking them into the rice mixture. (Place the mussels and clams hinge side down, so they can open easily.) Place the skillet on the bottom rack of the oven and cook for 15 minutes—do not stir. Quickly

sprinkle the peas on top and place the skillet back in the oven for 10 minutes more, or until all of the liquid has been absorbed. Cover with a dish towel and let rest for 5 minutes before serving. Garnish with the parsley and lemons.

NOTE: Smoked paprika is best for this recipe, but if you can't find it easily, you can substitute regular paprika.

1 pound fresh mussels, scrubbed and debearded
1 pound clams, scrubbed
½ pound medium prawns, tails left on, peeled and deveined (thawed if frozen)
½ cup frozen peas, thawed

1 tablespoon chopped fresh parsley, for garnish
2 lemons, cut lengthwise into wedges, for garnish

tamale pie

For a long time we were on the search for the perfect tamale pie. Here, we've added ground beef, chili, our favorite Muir Glen tomatoes, and fresh spices. For a vegetarian option, you can use vegetarian chili and more corn, red peppers, and onion. It's a one-pan meal! Serve it with your favorite hot sauce or salsa.

MAKES 8 SERVINGS

* Position a rack in the center of the oven and preheat to 400°F.

* Prepare the Moist Cornbread batter on page 133, but do not bake it. Set batter aside and continue with this recipe.

* To prepare the filling, heat a 10-inch cast iron skillet over medium-high heat. Add the ground beef, cumin, chili powder, paprika, red pepper flakes, cayenne, oregano, salt, and pepper and cook, stirring occasionally, until the beef is browned. Transfer to a plate.

* Reduce the heat to medium. Add the oil and butter to the skillet. When the butter has melted, add the onion and bell pepper and cook, stirring occasionally, until the onion is softened but not browned, about 4 minutes. Add the garlic and cook 2 minutes longer.

* Add the beef back to the skillet with the onion mixture. Add the tomatoes, chili, chiles, and corn.

* Sprinkle the cheddar cheese over the top. Pour the cornbread batter over the top of the cheese, spreading it evenly with a spatula. Transfer the skillet to the oven and bake for 15 minutes. Lower the heat to 350°F, remove the pan from the oven, and drizzle the melted butter over the top. Return

(continued)

Moist Cornbread batter (see recipe on page 133)

FILLING

1 pound lean ground beef

1 teaspoon ground cumin

2 teaspoons chili powder

1 teaspoon smoked paprika

½ teaspoon crushed red pepper flakes

¼ teaspoon cayenne pepper (optional, for more heat)

½ teaspoon dried oregano

½ teaspoon kosher salt, or ¼ teaspoon fine salt

Freshly ground black pepper

1 tablespoon olive oil

1 tablespoon butter

1 white onion, diced

1 red bell pepper, seeds and ribs removed and finely chopped

2 cloves garlic, minced

1 (14.5-ounce) can Muir Glen fire-roasted crushed tomatoes (see note, page 71)

2 (14.5-ounce) cans of your favorite mild or hot chili

3 roasted poblano chiles, skinned, seeded, and diced (see method on page 40), or 3 tablespoons diced green chiles (optional)

2 cups fresh or frozen corn,
thawed and drained if frozen
2 cups grated sharp cheddar
cheese
2 tablespoons melted salted
butter

Sour cream, for serving
¼ cup chopped fresh cilantro
¼ cup chopped green onions
1 avocado, peeled, pitted,
and diced

the skillet to the oven and continue to bake until the top is nicely browned and a toothpick inserted in the center comes out clean, 20 to 25 minutes. Remove from the oven and let stand for 10 minutes. Cut into wedges and serve with sour cream, cilantro, green onions, and avocado.

bernie's cabbage rolls

Bernie and Bob Manofsky shared this recipe, which has been passed down in their family for three generations, with us. We cooked it together during a visit, and it immediately became part of our family's repertoire.

MAKES ABOUT 16 ROLLS

* Position a rack in the center of the oven and preheat to 350°F.

* Set the cabbages down on a cutting surface so that the base is facing up. Insert a long knife just next to the core and cut all around it, removing the large end of the core. Add water to a large saucepan to a depth of 2 inches. Place the cabbages in a steamer basket in the pan, cover, bring to a boil, and steam until the leaves are soft enough to be removed, about 3 minutes. Separate the large outer leaves and let cool on paper towels; you will use only 6 large outer leaves per head. Slice the rest of 1 head of cabbage and place in the bottom of a 12-inch cast iron skillet. (Save the other head of cabbage for another use.)

* In a medium bowl, combine the beef, pork, rice, onion, garlic, cinnamon, salt, pepper, and tomato juice. Mix well.

* Place ⅓ cup of the meat mixture on the stem end of each cabbage leaf. Roll once, and then fold in the sides and continue to roll. Place seam side down in the skillet on top of the sliced cabbage. Repeat until all of the meat mixture is used.

* Pour in the chicken broth, cover with foil, and bake for 50 minutes. Carefully remove pan from the oven and drain off half of the liquid. Spoon the tomatoes evenly over the cabbage rolls. Replace the foil and bake for 10 minutes longer.

* Serve from the skillet, and top each roll with sour cream.

2 heads green cabbage
1 pound lean ground beef
½ pound lean ground pork
½ cup uncooked long-grain rice
½ yellow onion, grated (about ½ cup)
1 clove garlic, minced
1 teaspoon ground cinnamon
2 teaspoons salt
1 teaspoon freshly ground black pepper
½ cup tomato juice
3 cups chicken broth
1 (14.5-ounce) can diced tomatoes, drained

Sour cream, for serving

cornish pasty

The Welsh copper miners in Butte, Montana, carried meat pies in their lunch pails. Baked in a skillet and served for dinner with a green salad, they're a way we celebrate our family's Montana roots. The meat pies look like large, golden-brown turnovers.

MAKES 4 SERVINGS

PASTRY
2 cups all-purpose flour
½ teaspoon salt
¾ cup vegetable shortening
½ cup very cold water

FILLING
1 to 2 russet potatoes, peeled
    and cut into ½-inch cubes
    (about 3 cups)
¾ cup chopped yellow onion
    (about ½ onion)
1 pound top sirloin, cut into
    ½-inch cubes
2 teaspoons salt
½ teaspoon freshly ground
    black pepper
2 tablespoons salted butter

Ketchup, for serving

❋ To prepare the pastry, mix together the flour and salt in a large bowl. With your fingers or a pastry cutter, mix in the shortening until the mixture has the consistency of coarse cornmeal. Add the water 2 tablespoons at a time and stir with a fork until the dough just starts to come together. Form the dough into a ball, divide in half, and shape each half into a flat disk, ½ inch thick. Cover the halves with plastic wrap and chill in the refrigerator while you prepare the filling.

❋ To prepare the filling, in a large bowl, mix together the potatoes, onion, and sirloin. Season with the salt and pepper.

❋ Position a rack in the center of the oven and preheat to 400°F.

❋ On a well-floured surface, roll out one dough half into a 10-inch circle. Spread half of the filling over half of the circle, leaving a 1-inch border. Cut 1 tablespoon of the butter into pieces and dot the filling with the butter. Gently pull the top edge of the dough over the filling to meet the bottom edge in a half-moon shape, flatten gently, and fold the bottom of the dough up over the edge. Be sure to leave about a ½-inch border to seal tightly. Crimp the edge with the tines of a fork, pressing the dough carefully. Cut a few small vents in the top of the pastry with the tip of a sharp knife. Gently transfer the pie to a lightly buttered 12-inch cast iron skillet.

Repeat with the other dough half, remaining filling, and butter. Carefully place the second pie in the skillet.

* Place the skillet in the oven and bake the pies for 50 minutes. Cut the pies in half and transfer carefully to dinner plates. Serve warm with ketchup for dipping.

classic grilled reubens

Reubens are named after Arthur Reuben, who created this delicious sandwich in his New York deli in 1941. We bet he didn't realize it would still be such a hit today. New York's Katz's Delicatessen is still our favorite place to get a true Reuben. Sometimes we slice these sandwiches into eighths and serve as an appetizer. A crispy kosher pickle makes a perfect finishing touch.

MAKES 2 SANDWICHES

❋ To prepare the dressing, in a small bowl, add all the ingredients and mix well. Set aside.

❋ To prepare the sandwiches, spread 3 tablespoons of dressing on each slice of bread. On the 2 bottom slices, layer half the pastrami, 4 slices of pickle, half the sauerkraut, and 2 slices of cheese. Top with the other slices of bread.

❋ Heat a cast iron skillet or griddle over medium heat. Melt 2 teaspoons of the butter. Place the sandwiches in the pan and press down on them with a smaller skillet or the back of a spatula. Cook until golden brown, about 3 minutes. Use a spatula to remove the sandwiches to a plate. Melt the remaining butter in the skillet. Place the uncooked sides of the sandwiches facing down (use your hand to hold the sandwiches together while turning) in the pan, and cook until golden and the cheese has melted, about 3 minutes. Cut in half and serve with a crispy dill pickle or pepperoncini.

THOUSAND ISLAND DRESSING
½ cup mayonnaise

3 tablespoons ketchup

1 tablespoon white wine vinegar

½ teaspoon horseradish

1 teaspoon Worcestershire sauce

1 teaspoon lemon juice

2 tablespoons finely diced dill pickle

SANDWICHES
4 slices rye or dill rye bread

8 ounces pastrami or corned beef

2 dill pickles, cut lengthwise into ¼-inch slices

½ cup sauerkraut or coleslaw

4 slices Swiss cheese

4 teaspoons butter

Dill pickles or pepperoncinis, for serving

VEGETABLES
& SIDES

he cast iron skillet is such a perfect match for so many side dishes, it was hard to narrow down our list: potatoes, potatoes, potatoes! The skillet works magic on them. The Moist Cornbread, Herbed Skillet Bread, and Fennel-Ricotta Skillet Bread are naturals for cast iron. They come out light and fluffy with crispy, golden crusts. The caramelization that takes place with the Caramelized Shallots and the Ginger-Glazed Carrots makes them as good as candy.

These are the side dishes we most often prepare. Once you get a feeling for how the cast iron skillet browns and crisps vegetables and brings out their flavors, you can experiment with all kinds of vegetables. Choose whatever is in season and then sauté or caramelize it in your cast iron skillet, exploring new flavors along the way.

rosemary roasted potatoes

Crisp on the outside, creamy and soft on the inside, these potatoes are perfect alongside roast chicken.

MAKES 4 SERVINGS

* Position a rack in the center of the oven and preheat to 400°F.

* Cut each potato into 6 wedges. Toss with the olive oil and rosemary, coating them completely. Season with salt and pepper. Place in a 10- or 12-inch cast iron skillet, and put the skillet in the oven. Roast until crisp and golden, 30 to 40 minutes. Garnish with the parsley.

2½ pounds small Yukon Gold potatoes, scrubbed (but not peeled)
¼ cup extra-virgin olive oil
1 tablespoon chopped fresh rosemary
Sea salt
Freshly ground black pepper

1 tablespoon lightly chopped fresh parsley, for garnish

sweet potato soufflé

Sweet potatoes are simply underutilized. They tend to be relegated to Thanksgiving, and instead they should be included in our weekly repertoire. They are sweet, golden, and healthy.

MAKES 6 TO 8 SERVINGS

8 medium sweet potatoes or yams (about 4 pounds)
1 teaspoon salt
5 tablespoons salted butter, at room temperature
½ cup half-and-half
¼ cup apple cider
3 tablespoons packed light brown sugar
½ teaspoon ground cinnamon
1 teaspoon grated orange zest
3 tablespoons chilled salted butter, cut into small pieces

❧ Position a rack in the center of the oven and preheat to 350°F.

❧ Put the sweet potatoes in a large stockpot, cover with cold water, and add the salt. Bring to a boil over high heat. Reduce the heat to medium and cook the potatoes until soft when pierced, 30 to 40 minutes. Drain and allow to cool.

❧ Peel the sweet potatoes and place in a large bowl. Mash to a coarse consistency with a potato ricer or masher. Add the room-temperature butter, half-and-half, apple cider, brown sugar, cinnamon, and orange zest. Beat with an electric mixer on medium speed until fluffy, about 2 minutes.

❧ Transfer to a buttered 10- or 12-inch cast iron skillet. Dot the potatoes with the chilled butter pieces and bake in the oven until the top is golden brown, about 30 minutes. For a perfect golden crust on top, broil for the last 5 minutes.

NOTE: If prepared ahead of time, top with the butter pieces just before reheating.

rösti potatoes

This crisp potato pancake is a Kramis family tradition. We have strong family ties to Switzerland and have been enriched by family exchanges over the years. Our most memorable meals always include rösti with an assortment of sausages. You can also fry some diced prosciutto or pancetta and sprinkle it on top.

MAKES 6 SERVINGS

6 medium russet potatoes
¼ cup olive oil, divided
¼ cup (½ stick) butter, divided
½ cup grated Gruyère cheese

* In a large pot filled two-thirds full, bring water to a boil over medium-high heat. Add the potatoes and cook for 10 minutes. Strain the potatoes and set aside to cool for 30 minutes.

* Using a box grater or food processor fitted with a small grater, shred the potatoes.

* Heat 2 tablespoons of the oil and 2 tablespoons of the butter in a 10-inch cast iron skillet over medium-low heat. Add the grated potatoes and gently press down on them with a spatula, spreading them out to cover the entire pan. Cover and cook for 10 minutes, leaving the lid ajar or wrapping it with a lightly moistened tea towel (this will prevent moisture from dripping back onto the rösti). Remove the lid and cook for 10 minutes more, or until a golden crust forms.

* Preheat the broiler.

* Return the lid to the skillet. Using oven mitts, grasp the skillet and lid firmly with two hands and carefully turn the potatoes onto the lid. Add the remaining 2 tablespoons of oil and butter to the skillet, let the butter melt, and then carefully slide the rösti back into the skillet with the crisp side up; cook for 10 to 15 minutes longer, or until a golden crust forms. Scatter the Gruyère over the top, and then place the skillet under the broiler until the cheese has melted. Serve hot.

potato pancakes

So easy! So good! Serve these pancakes as an appetizer by making them smaller and topping them with sour cream and caviar. The cast iron skillet browns the pancake and forms a crisp crust on the outside. Top with whatever you like. We serve ours with applesauce for a sweeter version or chopped chives, chorizo, and green onions for a savory cake.

MAKES 4 SERVINGS (8 PANCAKES)

1 large egg
2 tablespoons grated yellow onion
3 tablespoons all-purpose flour
½ teaspoon salt
3 russet potatoes, peeled and placed in a bowl of cold water
6 tablespoons olive oil, divided

Sour cream, for serving
Chopped chives, for garnish

✻ Preheat the oven to 250°F.

✻ In a medium bowl, whisk the egg, add the grated onion, and mix. Add the flour and salt and whisk until blended.

✻ Remove the potatoes from the cold water and pat dry. Grate the potatoes on the medium-sized holes of a box grater. Place in a colander and rinse lightly with cold water. Press with paper towels to blot excess moisture. Add the grated potatoes to the egg mixture.

✻ Line a plate with paper towels. Heat 3 tablespoons of the oil over medium heat in a 12-inch cast iron skillet. Scoop ¼ cup of the potato mixture into the pan. Flatten with a spatula to a thickness of ¼ to ½ inch. Fry in batches, using the remaining oil, until golden, 4 to 5 minutes on each side. Remove to the paper towel–lined plate, and then transfer to a baking sheet and keep warm in the oven while you cook the remaining pancakes. Serve with sour cream and chives.

best baked beans

There's nothing like making your own baked beans. These beans have a wonderful blend of spices, without the high sodium content of canned beans. Although they take several hours to cook, you can just leave them unattended and let them slow-cook.

MAKES 12 SERVINGS

＊ In a large stockpot, bring the cold water to a boil over high heat. Add the beans to the boiling water and cook for 2 minutes. Remove from the heat, cover, and let soak for 1 hour. Drain in a colander and rinse the beans.

＊ Place a 10- or 12-inch cast iron skillet over medium heat. Add the bacon and cook until golden, turning once. Transfer the bacon to a paper towel. Pour off all but 3 tablespoons of the bacon fat.

＊ Return the skillet to medium heat. Add the onion and cook, stirring occasionally and scraping up the browned bits from the bacon, until golden brown. Add the beans, beer, water, molasses, maple syrup, Worcestershire sauce, brown sugar, dry mustard, and paprika. Coarsely chop the bacon and add it to the skillet. Reduce the heat to medium-low (or place the skillet in a 250°F oven) and cook, covered, for 3 hours. Add water as needed to keep the beans covered. During the last half hour of cooking, remove the lid and don't add any additional water to the beans. When the beans are done, stir in the salt just before serving.

8 cups cold water
2¾ cups (1 pound) dried Great Northern beans
4 strips bacon
½ yellow onion, diced
1 cup beer, preferably pale ale
2 cups water
½ cup molasses
¼ cup maple syrup
1 tablespoon Worcestershire sauce
2 tablespoons packed light brown sugar
2 teaspoons dry mustard
1 teaspoon paprika
2 teaspoons salt

elsie's zucchini pancakes

with Sour Cream Sauce

At the end of summer, if you're growing zucchini in your garden, you need recipes to use them all. (They seem to appear overnight.) We like to serve these zucchini pancakes with grilled chicken or fish.

MAKES 6 SERVINGS

SOUR CREAM SAUCE
¾ cup sour cream
2 tablespoons finely chopped green onion, both green and white parts
¼ cup dry white wine
1 tablespoon fresh lemon juice

ZUCCHINI PANCAKES
3 cups grated zucchini (about 4 medium-sized zucchini)
2 tablespoons all-purpose flour
2 tablespoons freshly grated Parmesan cheese
¼ cup finely chopped green onion, white and green parts (about 3 onions)
3 large eggs, beaten
1 tablespoon fresh lemon juice
1 tablespoon canola oil, plus more as needed

Finely chopped chives, for garnish

❈ To prepare the sauce, mix together the sour cream, green onion, wine, and lemon juice in a small saucepan and cook over medium heat just until warm. Reduce the heat to low while you prepare the pancakes.

❈ Preheat the oven to 250°F, and place a platter in the oven to warm.

❈ To prepare the pancakes, place the grated zucchini between two layers of paper towels and press lightly to remove some of the moisture. Transfer to a large bowl. Add the flour and mix to coat. Add the Parmesan cheese, green onions, eggs, and lemon juice and mix well.

❈ Heat 1 tablespoon canola oil in a 10- or 12-inch cast iron skillet over medium heat. Drop ⅓ cup of the pancake batter into the skillet for each pancake and cook, turning once, until golden brown on both sides, 2 to 3 minutes. Transfer to the warm platter in the oven and repeat until you have used all the batter, adding more oil to the skillet as needed.

❈ To serve, pour a little of the warm sauce over the pancakes and garnish with chopped chives.

skillet-roasted asparagus

Northwest asparagus appears in our farmers' markets in late March. This simple and delicious preparation captures the sweetness of the asparagus and offers a tasty alternative to the customary steaming. It's a perfect accompaniment to the first halibut of the season.

MAKES 4 SERVINGS

✢ Position a rack in the center of the oven and preheat to 400°F.

✢ Trim off the tough ends of the asparagus, or snap the asparagus where it naturally breaks. Place the spears in a 10- or 12-inch cast iron skillet. Pour the olive oil over the spears and, with your hands, turn the asparagus until it is evenly coated with oil. Sprinkle with the lemon zest and bake until tender, 12 to 15 minutes. Sprinkle with salt and pepper and serve in the warm skillet.

1 pound fresh asparagus spears, ½ inch thick
3 tablespoons extra-virgin olive oil
1 teaspoon lemon zest
Sea salt and freshly ground black pepper

roasted root vegetables

Straight from the garden to the skillet, there's nothing better than roasted vegetables. Lightly dressed, they are delicious served alongside salmon, halibut, roast chicken, or pork roast. Herbs de Provence adds a nice lavender flavor.

MAKES 6 SERVINGS

* Preheat the oven to 400°F.

* Put all the vegetables in a large bowl. Add the olive oil, herbs de Provence, thyme, orange zest and juice, and water, and toss, coating well.

* Transfer the vegetables to a 10- or 12-inch cast iron skillet, cover, and roast in the oven for 20 minutes. Uncover and cook until golden brown, 20 to 25 minutes more. Peel the beets and cut in half. Cut the parsnips and rutabaga in half lengthwise. Season the vegetables with salt and pepper, garnish with parsley, and serve.

6 shallots, peeled
2 to 3 small parsnips, scrubbed and root end trimmed
1 rutabaga, scrubbed and root end trimmed, cut into wedges
4 small golden and/or red beets, scrubbed and root end trimmed
2 small turnips, scrubbed and trimmed
1 fennel bulb, fronds trimmed, cut lengthwise into 1-inch slices
¼ cup olive oil
2 teaspoons herbs de Provence or Italian herbs
1 teaspoon fresh thyme leaves
1 tablespoon orange zest
2 tablespoons orange juice
3 tablespoons water

Salt and freshly ground black pepper
1 teaspoon chopped fresh flat-leaf parsley, for garnish

caramelized brussels sprout hash

with Crumbled Bacon

This is such a great way to cook brussels sprouts. The apple juice gives this dish its sweetness, and the lemon juice adds more flavor and helps the brussels sprouts retain their green color. It is a great accompaniment to any entrée. You can also add toasted hazelnuts or pecans for more texture.

MAKES 8 SERVINGS

3 strips thick-sliced bacon
   (optional)
3 tablespoon butter
2 cups sliced brussels sprouts,
   rinsed, ends slightly trimmed,
   and cut into ¼-inch slices
¼ cup apple juice or cider
¼ cup water
1 teaspoon lemon juice
¼ teaspoon lemon zest
Salt and freshly ground black
   pepper

* In a 10- or 12-inch cast iron skillet over medium heat, add the bacon strips and cook until crisp. Transfer the bacon to a plate lined with paper towels.

* Wipe out the skillet, and then add the butter. Once it has melted, add the brussels sprouts and cook for 2 minutes. Add the apple juice and water, cover, and cook for 3 minutes. Uncover, increase the heat to medium-high, and cook, gently stirring occasionally, for 3 minutes more, or until any moisture has been absorbed. Add the lemon juice. Reduce the heat to medium and cook for 5 minutes without stirring. Sprinkle the lemon zest over the brussels sprouts, season them with salt and pepper, and cook, carefully flipping the sprouts with a spatula from time to time, for 2 to 3 minutes, or until golden brown.

* Remove the pan from the heat, crumble the bacon over the brussels sprouts, and serve.

moist cornbread

We use this cornbread as the base for our Cornbread Pudding (page 139) because it doesn't crumble; it's also terrific on its own, served with melted butter and honey. For variety, try adding fresh herbs or ⅔ cup grated dry Jack, pepper Jack, or sharp cheddar cheese to the batter. We use Bob's Red Mill cornmeal—see Resources (page 189) for information.

MAKES 8 SERVINGS

＊ Position a rack in the center of the oven and preheat to 400°F.

＊ Generously butter the sides and bottom of an 8- or 10-inch cast iron skillet. In a large bowl, whisk together the cornmeal, flour, baking powder, baking soda, sugar, salt, and chili powder. In a medium bowl, whisk together the eggs, sour cream, half-and-half, 4 tablespoons of the melted butter (allow it to cool slightly before adding), and corn. Add the egg mixture to the cornmeal mixture and stir until just combined. Do not overmix.

＊ Heat the skillet over medium heat. Pour the cornmeal batter into the skillet, jiggling the skillet slightly to level out the batter.

＊ Bake in the oven for 10 minutes. Remove the skillet from the oven, and pour the remaining 2 tablespoons of melted butter over the top. Return to the oven and continue baking until golden brown and a toothpick inserted in the center comes out clean, about 10 minutes more. Cool. Cut into wedges and serve.

1 cup finely ground yellow cornmeal
1 cup all-purpose flour
1½ teaspoons baking powder
½ teaspoon baking soda
2 tablespoons granulated sugar
½ teaspoon salt
½ teaspoon chili powder
2 large eggs
½ cup sour cream
1 cup half-and-half
6 tablespoons butter, melted
⅔ cup fresh or frozen corn, thawed and drained if frozen

winter squash

with Cranberries, Hazelnuts, and Fried Sage

This is a great side dish to bring to holiday parties. The colors are so beautiful, and the flavors together make your squash taste delicious. Buying precut squash from the supermarket is a great time-saver. If you don't have time to fry sage leaves for garnish, just sprinkle the squash with a little fresh parsley.

MAKES 6 TO 8 SERVINGS

* Preheat oven to 375°F.

* In a large bowl, pour the butter and maple syrup over the squash. Add the salt, pepper, and dried cranberries and mix. Butter a 10-inch cast iron skillet. Transfer the squash to the skillet, cover with aluminum foil, and bake for 20 minutes.

* Meanwhile, line a plate with paper towels. In a 6- to 8-inch skillet, warm the oil over medium heat for 2 minutes, and then add the sage leaves, a few at a time. Fry for 1 to 2 minutes, and then remove with a slotted spoon to the paper towel–lined plate and quickly sprinkle with salt. Repeat with the rest of the sage leaves. Set aside.

* Remove the foil from the squash. With a large spoon or spatula, toss the squash and bake, uncovered, for 20 minutes more. Garnish with the hazelnuts and fried sage leaves and serve.

¼ cup melted butter, plus more for buttering the skillet

3 tablespoons maple syrup

1½ pounds winter squash, such as butternut or kabocha, peeled, seeded, and cut into 1-inch cubes (about 6 cups)

½ teaspoon salt

Freshly ground black pepper

½ cup dried cranberries

¼ cup vegetable oil

12 small to medium fresh sage leaves

½ cup hazelnuts, toasted and chopped, for garnish

herbed skillet bread

The aroma of freshly baked bread and rosemary fills your kitchen when this is in the oven. The cast iron skillet acts like a wood-burning oven and makes a wonderful crisp crust. This easy bread is excellent with roast chicken and ribs.

MAKES 8 SERVINGS

1 tablespoon sugar

1 cup warm water (105°F), divided

1 package active dry yeast

2¼ cups all-purpose flour, plus more as needed

2 teaspoons sea salt, divided

¼ cup plus 2 tablespoons olive oil, divided, plus more for drizzling

2 cloves garlic, thinly sliced

2 sprigs fresh rosemary, chopped

* In a large bowl, dissolve the sugar in ½ cup of the warm water. Sprinkle the yeast on top, and let it sit for 5 minutes. Add the remaining ½ cup water, the flour, ½ teaspoon of the salt, and ¼ cup of the olive oil. Stir with a wooden spoon until well blended and the mixture forms a soft dough.

* Turn the dough out onto a well-floured board and knead until smooth, about 5 minutes. Add additional flour as necessary to prevent the dough from sticking.

* Form the dough into a ball and place in a large, lightly oiled bowl. Turn to coat with the oil. Cover the bowl loosely with a damp tea towel, and let the dough rise for 45 minutes.

* Coat the bottom and sides of a 10-inch cast iron skillet with 1 tablespoon of olive oil. Place the dough in the skillet and press it evenly into the bottom of the pan. With a sharp knife, score the top lightly in a crisscross pattern. Brush with the remaining 1 tablespoon olive oil, and sprinkle the garlic and rosemary over the top. Sprinkle with the remaining 1½ teaspoons sea salt. Let rise for 30 minutes.

* While the bread is rising, position a rack in the center of the oven, and preheat the oven to 400°F.

* Place the skillet in the hot oven and bake for 20 to 25 minutes, until the crust is a light golden color. Remove from the pan right away and place on a wire rack to retain the crisp crust. Brush a little olive oil over the top, slice into wedges, and serve warm.

fennel-ricotta skillet bread

The ricotta cheese makes this bread very moist, and no kneading is required. Although it is simple to prepare, you will need to allow time for two separate risings, each taking an hour, so plan to make your bread on a relaxing day at home.

MAKES 8 SERVINGS

1 package active dry yeast
¼ cup warm water (105°F)
1 cup ricotta cheese, warmed to
    100°F to 110°F in a microwave
    oven
1 tablespoon butter
2 tablespoons sugar
1 teaspoon salt
¼ teaspoon baking soda
2 teaspoons fennel seed
1 egg
2 cups all-purpose flour

Butter, at room temperature, for
    topping
Sea salt, for topping

* In a small bowl, dissolve the yeast in the warm water for 5 minutes.

* In a large bowl, mix together the warm ricotta cheese, butter, sugar, salt, baking soda, fennel seed, and egg. Add the yeast mixture. Gradually add all the flour, ½ cup at a time, mixing well after each addition. The batter will be moist and slightly sticky. Remove from the bowl and form into a soft ball on a lightly floured surface.

* Rinse the bowl the dough was in, and then butter the bottom and halfway up the sides. Place the dough in the bowl and cover tightly with plastic wrap. Let rise for 1 hour.

* Push the dough down with the palm of your hand. Shape it evenly into a round, flat circle in a well-buttered 8-inch cast iron skillet. The dough should be touching the sides of the skillet. Cover with plastic wrap and let rise for 1 hour.

* While the bread is rising, position a rack in the center of the oven and preheat to 350°F.

* Remove the plastic wrap, place the skillet in the oven, and bake the bread until golden brown, 35 to 40 minutes. Remove from the oven, brush the top of the bread with soft butter, and sprinkle with sea salt. Then remove from the pan and cool on a baking rack. Cut into wedges and serve.

cornbread pudding

Tom Douglas, chef and owner of several of Seattle's top restaurants, inspired this savory pudding. We pair it with barbecued ribs or any slow-cooked meat or salmon. The cornbread stays moist on the inside, crispy and golden on the outside.

MAKES 6 SERVINGS

* Position a rack in the center of the oven and preheat to 350°F.

* Put the cubed cornbread in a buttered 10- or 12-inch cast iron skillet. Set aside. Warm the butter in another skillet over low heat, add the onions, and cook very slowly, stirring occasionally, until soft and golden brown, at least 20 minutes. Remove from the heat. Scatter the onions, cheese, parsley, rosemary, and thyme over the cornbread cubes. Whisk the heavy cream and eggs with the salt and pepper in a mixing bowl and pour over the cornbread cubes. Let sit for 10 minutes to allow the cornbread to absorb some of the custard. Bake until set and golden, about 40 minutes. Serve hot.

4½ cups cubed Moist Cornbread (page 133) or other cornbread (see note)

1 tablespoon unsalted butter

1 cup thinly sliced yellow onions (about ½ large onion)

¾ cup grated dry Jack cheese, cheddar, or Cougar Gold cheddar (see Resources, page 189)

2 teaspoons chopped fresh flat-leaf parsley

½ teaspoon chopped fresh rosemary

½ teaspoon chopped fresh thyme leaves

2 cups heavy cream

3 large eggs

1 teaspoon kosher salt

½ teaspoon freshly ground black pepper

NOTE: To save time, you can substitute cornbread made from a mix for our Moist Cornbread. Just be sure to let the cornbread cool completely before cutting it into cubes. For a more custard-like version of the pudding, increase the heavy cream to 3 cups and use 4 eggs.

ginger-glazed carrots

These carrots are a perfect example of why the cast iron skillet is so important in your kitchen. The tender carrots caramelize with the butter, ginger, and sugar, bringing out their sweetness.

MAKES 4 SERVINGS

1½ pounds carrots, peeled and cut into ½-inch slices or into a diagonal or V-cut
¾ cup water
¼ cup (½ stick) salted butter
1-inch piece fresh ginger, peeled and thinly sliced
2 tablespoons sugar

Sea salt
1 tablespoon chopped fresh parsley, for garnish

❖ Place the carrots, water, butter, ginger, and sugar in a 10-inch cast iron skillet. Bring to a boil over medium-high heat, reduce the heat to medium-low, simmer and cook for 10 minutes, stirring occasionally until the carrots are tender and a buttery sauce has developed. Season with sea salt, garnish with parsley, and serve immediately.

roasted carrots and fennel

with Fresh Dill

This is a simple roasted vegetable dish that looks as good as it tastes. It is great alongside fish or chicken. You could substitute golden beets for the carrots.

MAKES 4 TO 6 SERVINGS

* Preheat oven to 425°F.

* In a large bowl, toss the carrots and fennel with the melted butter. Sprinkle with salt and pepper, and toss again until the vegetables are well coated.

* Transfer the vegetables to a baking pan and bake for 15 minutes, stirring every 5 minutes, until the vegetables are easily pierced with a fork. Remove from the oven and sprinkle the vegetables with the dill and a little more salt before serving.

5 medium carrots, peeled and sliced ⅛ inch thick
2 fennel bulbs, sliced ⅛ inch thick
3 tablespoons butter, melted
Salt and freshly ground black pepper
1 tablespoon lightly chopped dill

sautéed green beans

with Melting Tomatoes and Pine Nuts

We love the crispiness of green beans paired with the sweet, soft burst of roasted tomatoes. This makes a great side dish for fish or roast chicken. You can also sprinkle some crumbled goat cheese on top before serving.

MAKES 6 SERVINGS

* Preheat oven to 350°F.

* In a medium bowl, gently toss the tomatoes together with the olive oil and ½ teaspoon of the herbs de Provence. Sprinkle with salt and pepper. Put the tomatoes in a 10- or 12-inch cast iron skillet and roast for 20 to 25 minutes, or until the tomatoes have shriveled slightly and have turned a deeper, darker color. Meanwhile, fill a large bowl with ice water, and set it aside. Bring a pot of lightly salted water to a boil, and add the green beans. Cook for 4 minutes, drain, and quickly add the beans to the ice water bath. When the beans have cooled, drain them well and set aside.

* Heat a 10- or 12-inch cast iron skillet over medium heat. (If you have only one skillet, you can wait until the tomatoes are done roasting, transfer them to a plate, and use the same skillet.) Add the butter and cook until it turns light brown, about 4 minutes. Add the green beans, the remaining ¼ teaspoon herbs de Provence, salt, and pepper and sauté for 4 to 5 minutes, until the beans are tender. Add the tomatoes back into the pan, sprinkle with the pine nuts and lemon zest, and serve.

12 ounces sweet baby tomatoes (red, yellow, or both), halved
1 tablespoon olive oil
¾ teaspoon herbs de Provence or Italian herbs, divided
Salt and freshly ground black pepper
2 pounds green beans, ends trimmed
2 tablespoons butter
3 tablespoons pine nuts, toasted
1 teaspoon lemon zest

stir-fried broccoli rabe

with Ginger-Sesame Sauce

We love the way broccoli rabe (also called rapini) absorbs the flavors of the sauce without getting mushy. If you can't find broccoli rabe, substitute broccoli, cutting the florets lengthwise but keeping the stalks intact.

MAKES 4 SERVINGS

2 to 3 tablespoons safflower or vegetable oil

2 cloves garlic, sliced

¼ teaspoon crushed red pepper flakes

2 bunches broccoli rabe, ends trimmed

½ cup water

GINGER-SESAME SAUCE

1 tablespoon oyster sauce

2 tablespoons soy sauce

2 teaspoons sugar

¼ teaspoon crushed red pepper flakes

1¼-inch-thick slice fresh ginger

½ cup water

1 teaspoon cornstarch

¼ teaspoon sesame oil

Cooked jasmine rice, for serving

✽ Warm the oil in a 10- or 12-inch cast iron skillet over medium heat. Add the garlic and red pepper flakes and cook for 30 seconds to 1 minute; then remove the garlic with a slotted spoon and reserve. Add the broccoli rabe and the water to the pan. Cover and simmer for 5 minutes. Remove the skillet from the heat, drain the excess liquid, and set aside. Mince the reserved garlic.

✽ To prepare the sauce, in a small saucepan over low heat, add the reserved garlic, oyster sauce, soy sauce, sugar, red pepper flakes, ginger, and water and stir. In a small bowl, combine the cornstarch with 2 tablespoons of cold water and stir. Add this to the oyster sauce and increase the heat to medium-high. As the sauce begins to boil, keep stirring and reduce the heat to medium. Stir until the sauce thickens, and then remove the pan from the heat and stir in the sesame oil.

✽ Return the skillet with the broccoli rabe to the stove over medium-high heat and pour about ½ cup of the sauce (or enough to coat) over the broccoli, tossing with tongs. Cook for 3 to 4 minutes, until the broccoli is tender. Serve with rice and extra sauce on the side.

caramelized shallots

The cast iron skillet caramelizes the shallots, leaving them soft and sweet. We love these shallots as a side dish for chicken and turkey. They also pair well with green beans or braised carrots.

MAKES 6 TO 8 SERVINGS

* Position a rack in the center of the oven and preheat to 400°F.

* Peel the shallots. Trim off the rough part of the root. Cut large shallot cloves in half. Place in a medium bowl. Add the olive oil, vinegar, salt, and brown sugar. Toss to coat.

* Place in a 10- or 12-inch cast iron skillet and cover with foil. Bake for 20 minutes. Remove the foil, gently toss the shallots, and continue baking until golden and soft, another 20 minutes.

10 to 12 whole shallot cloves
(1 shallot usually has 2 cloves)
¼ cup extra-virgin olive oil
¼ cup balsamic vinegar
½ teaspoon salt
3 tablespoons packed light
brown sugar

wild mushroom and caramelized red onion tarte tatin

If you are unable to get wild mushrooms, this tart works fine with a mix of cremini, button, and portobello mushrooms. And if you don't have time to make a pie crust, you can use frozen puff pastry—just roll it out and trim the corners to create a round pastry. This is a great appetizer with a crisp white wine.

MAKES 6 TO 8 SERVINGS

PIE CRUST
1½ cups all-purpose flour
½ teaspoon salt
6 tablespoons chilled unsalted butter, cut into cubes
2 tablespoons cold shortening
5 to 6 tablespoons ice water

FILLING
2 tablespoons olive oil, divided
2 tablespoons butter, divided
½ red onion, root end trimmed, peeled and cut into 6 to 8 (½-inch) wedges
1 teaspoon sugar
½ shallot, peeled and minced
8 cups assorted wild mushrooms, sliced
1 teaspoon fresh thyme
¼ teaspoon salt
Freshly ground black pepper
2 tablespoons Madeira, sherry, or balsamic vinegar
¼ cup heavy cream

❈ To prepare the pastry dough, in a large bowl, mix together the flour and salt. With a pastry knife or your fingers, add the butter and the shortening, working quickly to blend with the flour until the mixture resembles small peas. Do not overwork. Add 1 to 2 tablespoons ice water at a time and mix well, using your hands. Once you have added all of the water, form the dough into a ball or flat disk. Wrap it in plastic wrap and refrigerate for at least 1 hour. (Alternately, you can prepare the dough in a food processor: add the flour and salt, pulse once, and then add half of the butter and the shortening and pulse twice. Add the rest of the butter and shortening and pulse five times, or until the mixture resembles small peas. Add the water 1 to 2 tablespoons at a time, pulsing once or twice between each addition. Once you have added all of the water, form the dough into a ball or disk, wrap it in plastic wrap, and refrigerate for at least 1 hour.)

❈ To prepare the filling, place a rack in the upper third of the oven and preheat to 400°F.

❈ In a 10- or 12-inch cast iron skillet over medium heat, warm 1 tablespoon each of the olive oil and butter. Add the onion wedges and cook for 5 minutes. Flip the onions, sprinkle with the sugar, and cook for 5 minutes longer. Remove to a plate.

* Add the remaining tablespoon each of olive oil and butter to the pan. Add the shallots and cook for 2 minutes. Add the mushrooms and cook for 10 to 15 minutes, stirring occasionally. After the mushrooms have released their moisture and begun to brown, add the thyme, salt, and pepper. Continue to cook until the mushrooms start to turn golden brown. Add the Madeira and cook for 1 minute. Add the cream and cook for 2 minutes. Add the onion wedges back to the pan with the mushrooms. Remove the pan from the heat and set aside.

* On a lightly floured surface, roll out the dough into a circle. Place the dough on top of the filling, tucking it in if needed. Make three slits in the top to vent the tart while cooking. Place it on the upper rack and bake for 15 minutes, or until the tart is golden. Remove the skillet from the oven. Place a plate that is slightly larger than the skillet atop the skillet. Using two pot holders, grasp the skillet and plate tightly, quickly flip the skillet, and wait for about 5 seconds before carefully setting the plate on the counter and removing the skillet. If some filling remains in the skillet, place it back on the tart. Sprinkle with salt, garnish with thyme and blue cheese, and serve.

1 teaspoon fresh thyme, for garnish
¼ cup crumbled blue cheese, for garnish

sautéed swiss chard

with Caramelized Onions

The cast iron skillet works wonders with sautéed greens. It absorbs any excess liquid, leaving the greens tender but not mushy. Rich in flavor, this is an excellent accompaniment to pork, lamb, or chicken. We like to add toasted pine nuts or fresh pomegranate seeds for the holidays.

MAKES 6 SERVINGS

3 tablespoons salted butter, divided

1 sweet yellow onion, quartered and thinly sliced

1 teaspoon sugar

Salt

2 heads Swiss chard, rinsed, dried, and cut into 2-inch strips (stems removed)

4 tablespoons orange juice, divided

4 tablespoons apple cider, divided

¼ teaspoon freshly grated nutmeg, divided

Freshly ground black pepper

* Melt 1 tablespoon of the butter in a 10- or 12-inch cast iron skillet over medium heat. Add the onions and cook, stirring occasionally, for about 5 minutes. Add the sugar and a pinch of salt and continue cooking until caramelized, 5 to 10 minutes longer. Transfer to a plate.

* Working in two batches, add 1 tablespoon of the butter to the skillet and half of the Swiss chard. Stir in 2 tablespoons of the orange juice, 2 tablespoons of the apple cider, and ⅛ teaspoon of the nutmeg. Cook until the liquid starts to evaporate, about 10 minutes. Transfer to a bowl and cover with foil. (You can place the bowl in a 250°F oven to keep warm.) Repeat with the second batch of chard and the remaining butter, orange juice, cider, and nutmeg.

* Add the second batch of chard to the first batch. Add the cooked onions, season with salt and pepper, and toss to mix. Serve immediately.

warm swiss chard bread salad

This is a starch and a vegetable, all in one dish. The crisp bread cubes and warm wilted greens complement each other well.

MAKES 8 TO 10 SERVINGS

* To prepare the croutons, position a rack at the top of the oven and preheat the broiler. Toss the bread cubes with the olive oil in a large bowl. Spread the bread cubes in an even layer on a baking sheet and broil until golden brown, 3 to 5 minutes. Watch them carefully because they can easily burn. Flip the bread cubes over, and return the baking sheet to the oven for 3 minutes more to brown the other side. Remove from the oven and set aside.

* To prepare the salad, position a rack in the center of the oven and preheat to 350°F.

* Warm the olive oil in a 10- or 12-inch cast iron skillet over medium heat. Add the onions, leeks, and garlic. Cook, stirring occasionally, until softened, about 5 minutes. Stir in the Swiss chard, cover, and cook for 15 minutes. Add the beans and toss gently. Stir in the chicken stock, lemon juice, nutmeg, and salt and pepper to taste. Bring to a low boil. Spread the croutons on top, gently pressing them down into the mixture with a spatula. Pour the half-and-half over the croutons. Sprinkle the grated cheese evenly over the top of the croutons.

* Cover the skillet with foil and bake in the oven for 25 minutes. Remove the foil, turn on the broiler, and broil until the cheese is bubbly and golden brown, about 5 minutes more. Remove from the oven and let cool for 5 minutes before serving.

CROUTONS
8 ounces soft rustic bread, cut into 1-inch cubes (4 cups)
¼ cup extra-virgin olive oil

SALAD
2 tablespoons extra-virgin olive oil
1 yellow onion, chopped
3 large leeks, white and light green parts only, rinsed well and chopped
6 cloves garlic, minced
1 pound Swiss chard, de-ribbed and cut into 2-inch pieces
1 (14.5-ounce) can (1½ cups) cooked Great Northern beans or cannellini beans
1 cup chicken stock
Juice of 1 lemon
½ teaspoon freshly grated nutmeg
Salt and freshly ground black pepper
½ cup half-and-half
2 cups (8 ounces) grated Swiss or Gruyère cheese

seared tofu
with Fried Shallots and Ginger-Garlic Sauce

Our kids really enjoy tofu, whether it's fried, as in the Japanese dish *agedashi* tofu, in soups like miso, or pan-seared in a skillet until golden brown. Also known as bean curd, it is a great source of protein and very low in fat. It will absorb any flavors you add to it. Tofu ranges in firmness from soft to extra-firm. For this recipe, I like to use firm or extra-firm tofu.

MAKES 6 TO 8 SERVINGS

GINGER-GARLIC SAUCE
1 clove garlic, finely chopped
1 green onion, end trimmed, white and green parts finely chopped
¼ teaspoon peeled grated fresh ginger
1 teaspoon Korean hot pepper flakes or crushed red chili flakes, crushed (or pulsed briefly in a spice grinder)
2 tablespoons soy sauce
2 teaspoons rice wine vinegar
2 teaspoons sugar
1 teaspoon sesame oil

¼ cup vegetable or safflower oil
1 (1-pound) container firm or extra-firm tofu, rinsed, halved, and sliced ⅓ inch thick
1 teaspoon toasted sesame seeds, for garnish

❋ In a small bowl, mix the garlic, green onion, and ginger. Add the pepper flakes, soy sauce, rice wine vinegar, sugar, and sesame oil, and mix well. Set aside.

❋ Dry the tofu with paper towels to absorb excess moisture. Warm the vegetable oil in a 10- or 12-inch cast iron skillet over medium heat. When the oil is hot, add as many tofu pieces as you can fit in the pan without overcrowding (10 to 12). Fry on one side until golden, 5 to 7 minutes, and then flip the tofu with a spatula and cook for 5 minutes more, moving the pieces around in the pan to cook evenly. Using a slotted spoon, remove the tofu and gently dab it on a paper towel to absorb excess oil, and then place it on a serving plate, fanning the pieces out in a row. To serve, spoon the sauce over the tofu and garnish with the sesame seeds.

NOTE: You can also cube the tofu slices after searing and add them to a skillet of sautéed vegetables, such as broccoli or broccoli rabe, snow peas, and sliced red pepper. First, add some of the Ginger-Garlic Sauce to the veggies, cover the skillet, and cook for a few minutes, and then gently mix in the cubed tofu and serve.

spicy pork

with Sweet-and-Sour Eggplant

We love to use the smaller Chinese eggplants for this dish. They stay firm and hold their shape, and absorb the wonderful flavors. If you like things really spicy, you can add more Sriracha or red pepper flakes. This dish is great alongside sautéed greens or added to soba noodles.

MAKES 4 TO 6 SERVINGS

＊ To prepare the sauce, in a large bowl, mix together the broth, soy sauce, balsamic vinegar, sugar, and bean sauce. In a small bowl, mix together the water and cornstarch, and then add it to the sauce. Set aside.

＊ Place a 10- or 12-inch cast iron skillet over medium heat. Add the sausage and cook, using the back of a fork to flatten and break it up, for 5 minutes, or until browned. Remove to a plate and set aside.

＊ Without wiping out the skillet, add the oil over medium-low heat. When the oil is hot, add the ginger, red pepper flakes, and garlic and cook for 2 minutes. Remove the garlic and discard. Add the eggplant and, using tongs, sauté for about 2 minutes. Add the ground pork back into the skillet. Pour the sauce evenly over the pork and eggplant. Add the chili paste and sesame oil and mix, coating the pork and eggplant with the sauce. Cook for 5 minutes. Transfer to a platter, garnish with the green onions, and serve.

SWEET-AND-SOUR SAUCE

¼ cup chicken broth

3 tablespoons soy sauce

2 teaspoons balsamic vinegar

2 teaspoons sugar

1 tablespoon spicy black bean garlic sauce (optional)

2 tablespoons water

1 teaspoon cornstarch

½ pound spicy ground pork sausage

3 tablespoons vegetable or grapeseed oil

2 teaspoons peeled and minced fresh ginger

¼ teaspoon crushed red pepper flakes (optional)

1 clove garlic, peeled and smashed

2 Chinese eggplants or 1 large globe eggplant, ends trimmed and cut into strips 2 inches long and 1 inch thick

1 teaspoon Sriracha sauce or sambal oelek

½ teaspoon sesame oil

2 tablespoons chopped green onions, for garnish

OUTDOOR COOKERY

Cooking outdoors doesn't have to be a rugged experience. Whether we are camping in the woods or grilling on the backyard barbecue, we like to keep it simple. Summertime family gatherings at the beach are the perfect setting for the one-pot Seafood Bake cooked on a grate over a fire pit. The Arroz con Pollo and Cast Iron Chili are also one-pot meals that are sure to satisfy a hungry family after a day spent outdoors. When you are planning a camping trip, just prepare your ingredients ahead and store them in resealable plastic bags. When you're ready to cook, dinner will come together quickly.

Cast iron Dutch ovens and skillets—and all of these recipes—work equally well on outdoor grills or on a grate over an open fire. The best way to test the heat of an open fire is with your hand. Hold it about 3 inches above the fire, and time how long you can keep it there before you are forced to pull it away.

* 1 to 2 seconds: high heat. Best for searing meat and grilling shrimp.

* 3 to 5 seconds: medium heat. Best for most types of fish.

* 6 to 7 seconds: low heat. Perfect for grilling vegetables and slow-cooking dishes.

An outdoor meal wouldn't be complete without s'mores, so don't forget to pack the graham crackers, marshmallows, and chocolate bars along with your cast iron skillet.

skillet-roasted clams

with Garlic and Parsley

We love to dig clams at our family beach house in South Puget Sound. We can gather a large bucket of small Manila clams in 15 minutes and enjoy them later for dinner.

MAKES 4 SERVINGS

❋ Place the butter, garlic, and red pepper flakes in a cast iron Dutch oven over medium heat (or on a grate over a medium-heat fire). Melt the butter and simmer for 2 minutes. Add the wine, water, lemon juice, and clams. Stir to coat the clams. Cover and cook until all of the clams have opened, about 5 minutes. Sprinkle the parsley over the top and serve in shallow bowls with crusty French bread for dipping.

¼ cup (½ stick) butter
2 cloves garlic, minced
1 to 2 teaspoons crushed red pepper flakes
¼ cup dry white wine
¼ cup water
Juice of 1 lemon
4 pounds small steamer clams, soaked and rinsed

2 tablespoons chopped fresh parsley, for garnish
Crusty French bread, for serving

seafood bake

An incredible one-pot meal! Feel free to toss in whatever kind of seafood is fresh and available. While at the beach, we have everyone pick up a pint of blackberries to make cobbler. While we are eating dinner, it's baking away—the perfect dessert to follow a summer supper such as this.

MAKES 6 SERVINGS

3 tablespoons extra-virgin olive oil

1 pound kielbasa (Polish sausage), cut into 1-inch slices

1 fresh fennel bulb, trimmed, halved lengthwise, and thinly sliced crosswise

2 teaspoons fresh thyme

2 cloves garlic, finely chopped

1 medium yellow onion, coarsely chopped

1 cup dry white wine

1½ cups clam juice

1 (14.5-ounce) can chopped tomatoes, drained

2 teaspoons Old Bay Seasoning

½ teaspoon crushed red pepper flakes

3 ears corn, husked and snapped in half

Grated zest of ½ lemon

10 small red potatoes (about 1 pound), cooked

2 pounds mussels, scrubbed and debearded

2 pounds clams, rinsed

2 (2-pound) crabs, cooked, cleaned, top shell removed, and body cut into quarters, keeping legs attached

Juice of 1 lemon

¼ cup coarsely chopped fresh parsley

Salt and freshly ground black pepper

Lemon wedges, for garnish

Crusty loaf of bread, for serving

❋ Heat a 6- to 8-quart Dutch oven over the stove top or open fire using medium-high heat (see heating method on page 154).

❋ Combine the olive oil, kielbasa, fennel, thyme, garlic, and onions in your Dutch oven and cook for 10 minutes, stirring occasionally. Add the wine, clam juice, tomatoes, Old Bay Seasoning, and red pepper flakes, and stir. If cooking over a fire, bring to a boil directly over a medium-high heat. Then move the Dutch oven off to the side for indirect heat. Cover and cook for 10 minutes.

❋ Add the corn and lemon zest and cook for 5 minutes. Add the cooked potatoes, mussels, clams, and crabs; cover and cook until the mussels have opened, 5 minutes more. Squeeze the lemon juice over the top, sprinkle with parsley, and season with salt and pepper. Serve in large individual bowls with lemon wedges and a crusty loaf of bread.

cast iron chili

After skiing or just relaxing on a crisp, cool day, nothing's better than a hot pot of chili on the stove. It's not heavy—the simplicity of the recipe makes it a longtime favorite. It works equally well over a campfire or on your kitchen stove. Top with cheddar cheese and sour cream and serve with a basket of Moist Cornbread (page 133).

MAKES 6 SERVINGS

❋ Warm the oil in a cast iron Dutch oven over medium heat on a grill or on a grate over a medium-heat fire (see heating method on page 154). Add the onions and cook, stirring often, for 5 minutes. Add the garlic and stir. Add the ground beef, stirring to crumble the meat while it browns. After the meat browns, add the green peppers and cook for 2 minutes more. Stir in the chili powder, paprika, cumin, kidney beans, and red pepper flakes. Add the diced tomatoes with juice and the crushed tomatoes. Stir well and simmer for 15 minutes. Serve in bowls, topped with sour cream, chopped green onions, and grated cheddar cheese.

2 tablespoons vegetable oil
1 cup chopped yellow onion
2 cloves garlic, minced
1 pound lean ground beef
¾ cup chopped green bell pepper
1 tablespoon chili powder
½ teaspoon paprika
½ teaspoon ground cumin
2 (15.25-ounce) cans kidney beans, drained and rinsed
1 teaspoon crushed red pepper flakes
1 (28-ounce) can diced tomatoes, with their juice
1 cup canned crushed tomatoes

Sour cream, for serving
Chopped green onions, for serving
Grated cheddar cheese, for serving

herb-stuffed, pan-fried golden trout

Bring your cast iron skillet on your next fishing trip, and ideally you will catch something you can cook in it. Fresh trout will never taste better. Trout is very easy to cook and eat because it has just one big bone that can quickly be removed. Relax by the river, take in the view, and enjoy the wonderful flavors of your fresh catch. Potato salad is a perfect accompaniment (see page 95).

MAKES 2 SERVINGS

* Rub the trout inside and out with 2 tablespoons of the olive oil and sprinkle with the half of the salt and pepper. Line the inside of the trout with 3 to 4 lemon slices, and then tuck in the thyme, rosemary, and dill so that the fish becomes aromatic. Mix together the flour, cornmeal, paprika, and the rest of the salt and pepper in a shallow dish. Lightly coat the fish with the flour mixture.

* Warm the remaining 3 tablespoons olive oil in a 10- or 12-inch cast iron skillet over medium-high heat on a grill or on a grate over a medium-heat fire (see heating method on page 154). Place the trout in the skillet and cook for 5 minutes. Turn over and cook for another 5 minutes. Transfer to a plate.

* To prepare the sauce, in the same skillet, melt the butter over medium heat, add the shallot, and cook for 2 to 3 minutes. Remove the skillet from the heat and add the thyme, chives, and parsley.

* Open the fish like a book and remove the bone, which should come out easily, starting at the head. You can remove the skin or leave it on. To serve, drizzle the herb butter and a squeeze of lemon juice over the trout.

1 large or 2 small fresh trout, cleaned
5 tablespoons olive oil, divided
1 teaspoon salt
1 teaspoon freshly ground black pepper
1 or 2 lemons, cut into ½-inch circles
6 sprigs fresh thyme
4 to 6 large sprigs fresh rosemary
6 to 8 sprigs fresh dill or fennel
½ cup all-purpose flour
½ cup cornmeal
1 teaspoon paprika

HERB SAUCE
3 tablespoons butter
1 shallot, peeled and finely diced
1 teaspoon fresh thyme
1 tablespoon chopped chives or green onion
3 tablespoons chopped parsley

arroz con pollo

This classic Mexican one-dish meal is especially wonderful on a camping trip. Simplify your campsite preparation by chopping all the vegetables in advance and premeasuring the spices and rice. Transport everything in resealable plastic bags. Then assemble and cook in your Dutch oven. The rice turns a beautiful golden color from the saffron and paprika. The chicken is juicy, and the peppers add nice flavor.

MAKES 4 TO 6 SERVINGS

2 tablespoons olive or vegetable oil

1 large fryer chicken, cut into 8 pieces (or 2 bone-in skinless breasts, 2 drumsticks, and 2 skinless thighs)

2 large white onions, coarsely chopped

2 bell peppers (1 red, 1 green), seeds and ribs removed and coarsely chopped

2 cloves garlic, minced

1 (14.5-ounce) can diced tomatoes, with their juice

2 cups chicken stock

1 teaspoon paprika

Pinch saffron (optional)

Salt and freshly ground black pepper

2 cups uncooked long-grain white rice

Juice of 1 lemon

✻ Melt the oil in a cast iron Dutch oven over a medium-heat fire or over medium heat on a camp stove. Add the chicken and cook, turning occasionally, until lightly browned on all sides. Transfer to a plate.

✻ Add the onions and bell peppers and cook, stirring occasionally, for 10 minutes. Stir in the garlic and cook for 1 minute. Add the tomatoes, chicken stock, paprika, saffron, salt, and pepper. Cook for 5 minutes. Stir in the rice. Add the chicken to the pan and spoon the sauce over the chicken, submerging it as much as possible. Cook very slowly over a low- to medium-heat fire, or over low heat on a camp stove for approximately 45 minutes. Occasionally, turn the chicken gently and turn the pot to move the rice, but do not stir. Season to taste with additional salt, pepper, and lemon juice and serve.

NOTE: To add extra flavor, remove 2 chorizo sausages from their casings, add to the pan, and cook until browned before you brown the chicken. Add the sausage to the vegetable mixture when you add the chicken.

DESSERTS

pside-down cakes, Bread Pudding with Grand Marnier Sauce, Old-Fashioned Peach Dumplings, and Sautéed Bananas in Rum are classic examples of desserts that are perfect for the cast iron skillet because it conducts heat so evenly. Fruit caramelizes beautifully, crusts bake to golden, flaky perfection, and cakes come out light and moist. The Plum Galette and Bing Cherry Clafouti have a rustic feel when served in the hot skillet. Others, such as the Tarte Tatin and the Warm Pear-Ginger Upside-Down Cake are meant to be served right side up on a platter so that everyone can see the beautiful caramelization and symmetry of the apples and pears.

sautéed bananas in rum

Cactus restaurant in Seattle's Madison Park neighborhood is the source of this delicious dessert. Serve in individual dessert dishes and top with vanilla ice cream.

MAKES 4 SERVINGS

✻ Melt the butter in an 8-inch cast iron skillet over medium heat. Add the brown sugar and cook, stirring constantly, until the sugar has completely dissolved. Whisk in the rum just until combined. Put the banana quarters flat side down in the skillet and cook until golden, 2 to 3 minutes. Turn over and cook for 2 minutes more. Bring the skillet to the table and serve the bananas in bowls with vanilla ice cream.

¼ cup (½ stick) butter, cut into pieces
½ cup packed light brown sugar
3 tablespoons Myers's dark rum
2 ripe medium-sized bananas, peeled and halved crosswise, and then lengthwise

Coconut or Mexican vanilla ice cream, for serving

warm pear-ginger upside-down cake

We love adding cornmeal to baked goods and pancakes. It gives cakes more substance and texture and, when mixed first with hot water, makes them incredibly moist. The hint of ginger in this cake really pulls all the flavors together. Topped with fresh whipped cream or vanilla ice cream, this is the ideal finish to a winter's feast.

MAKES 8 TO 10 SERVINGS

* Position a rack in the center of the oven and preheat to 350°F.

* Melt 2 tablespoons of the butter in a 10-inch cast iron skillet over medium heat. Add ¼ cup of the sugar, stir just enough to combine, and cook without disturbing until the sugar dissolves and starts to turn golden brown (caramelize), about 5 minutes. Beginning with the outside edge and working your way toward the center in a circular pattern, arrange the pear slices on top of the caramelized sugar. Sprinkle the ginger and nutmeg over the top. Cook until the pears are soft and the caramel starts to thicken, about 5 minutes more. Remove from the heat and set aside.

* In a small bowl, whisk together the flour, baking powder, and salt. Place the cornmeal in a large bowl, add the boiling water, and stir to blend. Add the remaining 6 tablespoons butter and the remaining ½ cup sugar to the cornmeal mixture and mix until well blended. (This can be done by hand.) Beat in the eggs and vanilla. Beat in the flour mixture, a little at a time, alternating it with the milk, making sure not to overmix. Pour the batter on top of the pears in the skillet.

(continued)

8 tablespoons (1 stick) unsalted butter, at room temperature, divided
¾ cup sugar, divided
2 pounds firm but ripe Bartlett or Anjou pears (about 4 pears), peeled, cored, and cut into eighths
2 tablespoons minced candied ginger
¼ teaspoon freshly grated nutmeg
1 cup all-purpose flour
2 teaspoons baking powder
¼ teaspoon salt
⅓ cup medium-ground yellow cornmeal
½ cup boiling water
2 large eggs
1 teaspoon vanilla extract
½ cup whole milk

✻ Transfer the skillet to the oven and bake until the top starts to brown and the center of the cake feels firm and springs back when pressed, 18 to 20 minutes. Let the cake cool for 5 minutes. Run a knife around the edge to loosen it, and place an inverted plate on top of the skillet. Protecting both hands with oven mitts, flip the cake onto the plate. Replace any fruit that may have stuck to the skillet. Serve warm or at room temperature.

tarte tatin

(Upside-Down Apple Tart)

A classic French dessert, tarte tatin was meant to be cooked in a cast iron skillet. The apples caramelize perfectly and make a beautiful presentation when the tart is inverted.

MAKES 8 SERVINGS

* To prepare the pastry, sift the flour, salt, and sugar into a medium bowl. Rub the butter into the flour mixture with your fingers until it resembles coarse crumbs. Sprinkle the water into the mixture, and gently work it into the dough just until the dough holds together. Form into a ball, wrap in plastic wrap, and refrigerate for 30 minutes or overnight.

* To prepare the filling, scatter the butter pieces evenly over the bottom of a 10-inch cast iron skillet. Sprinkle the sugar evenly over the butter, covering the pan bottom. Arrange the apples tightly together in the skillet in a circular pattern, starting at the outside and working toward the center. The apple halves should be on their sides, holding each other up and all facing the same direction. Place 2 halves in the center of the pan. (During cooking, the apples will slide down more into the pan.)

* Place the skillet over medium-low heat and cook, uncovered, until the sugar begins to caramelize (turn golden brown), 35 to 40 minutes. During cooking, spoon some of the caramelized juices over the apples to help caramelize them.

* Position a rack in the center of the oven and preheat to 400°F.

(continued)

PASTRY

1 cup all-purpose flour
½ teaspoon salt
1 tablespoon sugar
6 tablespoons unsalted butter, cut into small pieces
3 tablespoons ice-cold water

FILLING

1 cup (2 sticks) unsalted butter, cut into small pieces
1½ cups sugar
8 to 9 apples (Jonagold, Fuji, or Golden Delicious), peeled, cored, and halved

Freshly whipped cream or ice cream, for serving

✳ Remove the pastry dough from the refrigerator and roll out on a lightly floured surface into a 12-inch circle. Drape the pastry dough over the apples, tucking the excess dough into the skillet without disturbing the apples. Place the skillet on a baking sheet in the oven, and bake until the pastry is golden brown, 20 to 25 minutes.

✳ Remove from the oven and let the tart sit for 3 minutes. Find a plate that is slightly larger than the skillet. Place it upside down on top of the skillet. Protecting both hands with oven mitts, grasp the cast iron skillet and the plate firmly with both hands, pressing the plate tightly onto the skillet. Invert the tart onto the plate. Replace any apples that may have stuck to the skillet. Serve with freshly whipped cream or ice cream.

old-fashioned peach dumplings

with Nutmeg Cream

Our good friend Jackie Clark gave us this recipe, and we are very grateful. We look for medium-sized, tree-ripened peaches to make our Old-Fashioned Peach Dumplings. The skillet provides the dry, even heat the dumplings need for a crisp crust and a juicy inside. We like to make this dessert in August when peaches are in full glory.

MAKES 8 SERVINGS

4 peaches

PASTRY
3 tablespoons sour cream
⅓ cup ice water
1 cup all-purpose flour
¼ cup cornmeal
2 teaspoons sugar
½ teaspoon salt
7 tablespoons cold, unsalted
   butter, cut into 8 pieces

SAUCE
¾ cup packed dark brown sugar
1½ cups water
¼ cup (½ stick) butter
½ teaspoon ground cinnamon
¼ cup granulated sugar

NUTMEG CREAM
1 cup chilled half-and-half
¼ cup granulated sugar
1 teaspoon freshly grated
   nutmeg

* Position a rack in the center of the oven and preheat to 375°F.

* Peel the peaches and cut them in half. Discard the pits.

* To prepare the pastry dough, whisk together the sour cream and ice water (removing the ice first) in a small bowl. Set aside.

* Place the flour, cornmeal, sugar, and salt in a large bowl. Mix with a whisk or your fingers until well combined. Add the butter. Mix with your fingers, with a pastry knife, or in a food processor until you have pea-sized pieces of butter (if using a food processor, quickly pulse 8 times). Add the sour cream mixture, 1 tablespoon at a time, gently mixing in after each addition. Once all of the liquid has been added, form the dough into a large disk. Do not handle the dough too much, and work quickly so that the butter stays cold. Wrap with plastic wrap and refrigerate for 1 to 2 hours.

* To prepare the dumplings, roll out the chilled dough on a lightly floured surface until you have a 12- to 14-inch

rectangle. With a sharp knife, cut the dough into 8 squares. Place a peach half in the middle of each square, bring the corners together, and pinch to seal. Try to enclose the fruit completely.

* To prepare the sauce, place the brown sugar, water, and butter in a 10-inch cast iron skillet and boil for 5 minutes over medium-high heat. Place the dumplings in the skillet with the sauce. Sprinkle the tops with the cinnamon and sugar. Place the skillet in the oven and bake for 30 minutes, until dumplings are lightly browned and you see juices beginning to leak out of them.

* While the dumplings are baking, prepare the Nutmeg Cream by combining the half-and-half, sugar, and nutmeg in a small bowl. Refrigerate until ready to serve.

* Remove the dumplings from the oven, set each on a plate, and serve with the chilled Nutmeg Cream.

cardamom-apricot financier

A *financier* is a French almond cake. Our good friend Jeremy Faber inspired this delicious recipe. He made individual financiers with an apricot dropped in the center of each and served them with cardamom ice cream. The flavors were so incredible that we added the cardamom directly to the cake and achieved a perfect crust by making one large cake in the cast iron skillet. Serve with vanilla ice cream.

MAKES 6 SERVINGS

* Place the almonds in a cast iron skillet and toast over medium heat until light brown. Using a food processor, pulse the almonds until finely ground. In a large bowl, combine the ground almonds, powdered sugar, flour, cardamom, salt, and orange zest. Whisk in the egg whites. Slowly stir in the ¾ cup melted butter. Cover the bowl with plastic wrap, and chill the batter in the refrigerator for 1 to 2 hours. (If you don't have this much time, you can instead place it in the freezer for 20 minutes.)

* Position a rack in the center of the oven and preheat to 425°F.

* Melt the 2 tablespoons butter over medium-low heat in a 10-inch cast iron skillet or four 6½-inch skillets. Tilt the pan to coat the bottom and sides. Pour the batter into the skillet, and drop the apricot halves on top (they will sink into the batter). Place the skillet in the oven, and bake until the dough just begins to rise, about 10 minutes. Reduce the heat to 400°F and continue baking until the cake begins to brown around the edges and on top, 7 to 8 minutes longer.

(continued)

1 cup slivered almonds
1⅔ cups powdered sugar
½ cup all-purpose flour
2 teaspoons ground cardamom
¼ teaspoon salt
Finely grated zest of 1 orange
6 large egg whites, lightly beaten (just until foamy)
¾ cup (1½ sticks) unsalted butter, melted
2 tablespoons unsalted butter for the pan
8 small apricots, quartered and pitted

Powdered sugar, for serving
Vanilla ice cream, for serving

* Turn off the oven, and let the cake stand in the oven until firm, about 10 minutes. Transfer the pan to a wire rack to cool completely.

* Invert the financier onto the wire rack. Reinvert it onto a platter and slice into wedges. Dust with powdered sugar and serve with vanilla ice cream.

bread pudding

with Grand Marnier Sauce

The top of this bread pudding gets perfect, crusty little peaks; the inside is soft and custardy. You can make this a day ahead and bake it while you are having dinner. Serve warm with the Grand Marnier Sauce.

MAKES 8 SERVINGS

* To prepare the bread pudding, butter a 10- or 12-inch cast iron skillet with 2 tablespoons of the butter. Layer half of the bread cubes, half of the raisins, half of the chopped pecans, and half of the peaches in the skillet. Repeat with the remaining bread cubes, raisins, pecans, and peaches.

* In a large bowl, beat the eggs until frothy. Add the milk, half-and-half, sugar, vanilla, Grand Marnier, cinnamon, nutmeg, and allspice. Whisk until well blended. Pour the egg mixture over the bread mixture in the skillet. Refrigerate for 1 hour, occasionally pressing down on the mixture gently to soak the bread cubes. Leave the bread cubes on top just lightly soaked with the egg mixture so that they will get slightly crispy when baked. Top the pudding with the remaining 4 tablespoons butter, cut into small pieces and distributed evenly over the top.

* Position a rack in the center of the oven and preheat the oven to 325°F. Place the skillet in the oven and bake for 1 hour. Remove from the oven and let cool for 30 minutes.

* While the bread pudding is cooling, prepare the sauce. Melt the butter in a heavy saucepan over medium heat. Add the sugar and cook, stirring constantly with a wooden spoon,

(continued)

6 tablespoons unsalted butter, divided
1 large French baguette or 10 slices French bread, cut into 1- to 2-inch cubes
½ cup raisins or dried cranberries (optional)
⅔ cup chopped pecans (optional)
2 cups fresh or frozen peaches (thawed if frozen), peeled, halved, and sliced
3 large eggs
2 cups whole milk
1 cup half-and-half
1 cup sugar
1 tablespoon vanilla extract
3 tablespoons Grand Marnier
⅛ teaspoon ground cinnamon
⅛ teaspoon freshly grated nutmeg
⅛ teaspoon ground allspice

GRAND MARNIER SAUCE
6 tablespoons unsalted butter
¾ cup sugar
¼ cup Grand Marnier
1 large egg

⅛ teaspoon freshly grated nutmeg, for serving

until the sugar has dissolved, about 2 minutes. Whisk in the Grand Marnier and cook for 1 to 2 minutes more. Remove from the heat.

* In a medium bowl, whisk the egg until frothy. Stir ¼ cup of the Grand Marnier mixture into the egg, and then add the tempered egg mixture to the saucepan. Return the pan to low heat and cook, whisking constantly, until the sauce begins to thicken, about 3 minutes. Remove the pan from the heat and continue whisking until the sauce is thick.

* Sprinkle the grated nutmeg over the bread pudding, and then cut the pudding into wedges and serve with the warm sauce. (You can pour the sauce over the top or serve it on the side.)

apple cake

with Caramel Frosting and Chopped Pecans

With its rich caramel frosting, this cake has the flavor of caramel apples. It's so easy to prepare; everything is mixed together in one bowl, and then baked, frosted, and served in the cast iron skillet.

MAKES 8 SERVINGS

2⅓ cups all-purpose flour
2 teaspoons baking soda
½ teaspoon salt
1 teaspoon ground cinnamon
¼ teaspoon ground nutmeg
½ cup unsalted butter
2 cups granulated sugar
2 eggs
4 cups peeled, grated apple
  (about 1½ pounds)

CARAMEL FROSTING
⅓ cup butter
½ cup packed light brown sugar
3 tablespoons whole milk
½ teaspoon vanilla extract
1½ cups powdered sugar

½ cup chopped pecans, for
  serving

* Position a rack in the center of the oven and preheat to 350°F. Butter a 10-inch cast iron skillet, dust with flour, and tap out the excess.

* To prepare the cake, combine the flour, baking soda, salt, cinnamon, and nutmeg in a large bowl and mix well. In a separate bowl, using an electric mixer, cream together the butter and sugar until smooth. Add the eggs, one at a time, beating well after each addition. Stir in the flour mixture until just combined. Fold in the apples.

* Spread the batter evenly in the skillet, and bake until a toothpick inserted in the center of the cake comes out clean, 40 to 45 minutes. Cool in the pan.

* To prepare the frosting, melt the butter in a small saucepan over medium heat. Add the brown sugar and stir until the sugar dissolves. Add the milk and bring to a boil. Pour into a mixing bowl and let cool for 10 minutes. Add the vanilla and powdered sugar and beat with a whisk until creamy. (The frosting will thicken as it cools.) Spread evenly over the cooled apple cake. Sprinkle the chopped pecans over the top and serve.

bing cherry clafouti

Clafouti is a French dessert similar to a Dutch baby but thicker and custard-like. It puffs up and gets golden in the skillet, and the cherries stay moist and sweet. We like to serve it for dessert or for a late weekend breakfast, warm with powdered sugar sprinkled over the top. Frozen Bing cherries, already pitted, make this a year-round favorite. We also like to substitute fresh apricots, pitted and quartered.

MAKES 6 SERVINGS

* Position a rack in the center of the oven and preheat to 400°F.

* Butter the bottom and sides of a 12-inch cast iron skillet. Place the cherries in the bottom of the pan, distributing evenly. In a medium bowl, mix the flour and sugar. Whisk in the milk, mixing until combined. Add the eggs, vanilla, Kirsch, nutmeg, and orange zest. Whisk until well combined. Pour all of the batter over the top of the cherries in the skillet. Dot the top with butter.

* Place the skillet in the oven and bake until puffed and golden, 25 to 30 minutes. Sprinkle with powdered sugar and serve.

1 (10-ounce) package (2 cups) frozen Bing cherries, thawed in a colander
1¼ cups all-purpose flour
⅓ cup granulated sugar
2¼ cups whole milk
4 eggs, lightly beaten
1 teaspoon vanilla extract
2 teaspoons Kirsch (cherry liqueur, optional)
¼ teaspoon freshly grated nutmeg
Zest of 1 orange
1 tablespoon butter, cut into small pieces

Powdered sugar, for garnish

skillet baked apples

with Caramel Sauce and Fleur de Sel

You know you are about to enjoy a relaxing and comfortable meal when you walk into a friend's home and spot a skillet of apples waiting to be baked. By the end of dinner, the smell of baking apples fills the air.

MAKES 6 SERVINGS

* To prepare the sauce, put the sugar in a medium saucepan over medium heat, and smooth it out to evenly cover the bottom. Cook without stirring until sugar starts to caramelize, about 5 minutes. When the sugar is a deep golden brown, remove the pan from the heat, add the butter, and then pour in the heavy cream (it will bubble quite a bit, and then settle into a rich brown caramel). Set aside.

* Position a rack in the center of the oven and preheat to 375°F.

* Place the apples in a 10- or 12-inch cast iron skillet. Mix the butter, brown sugar, and pecans in a small bowl. Place 3 marshmallows in the bottom of each apple (this will keep the filling from running out of the apple). Place 3 to 4 tablespoons of the butter mixture in the center of each apple. Cover and bake for 40 minutes. Serve warm in shallow dessert dishes with the chilled heavy cream poured around the apples. Drizzle ¼ cup of the caramel sauce over the apples. Garnish with a sprinkle of fleur de sel and the candied pecans.

CARAMEL SAUCE
1 cup sugar
3 tablespoons unsalted butter
¾ cup heavy cream
6 Jonagold apples, cored, top ¾ inch cut off, and peel removed 1 inch around the top
6 tablespoons butter, at room temperature
1 cup packed light brown sugar
½ cup chopped pecans
18 small marshmallows
½ cup chilled heavy cream

Fleur de sel or your favorite sea salt, for garnish
Chopped candied pecans, for garnish

plum galette

A galette is a free-form tart. You roll out the pastry and then fold the edges over the fruit. Served in the cast iron skillet, this rustic dessert, with its golden crust and shiny, glazed plums, makes a beautiful presentation at the table.

MAKES 6 TO 8 SERVINGS

PASTRY

⅓ cup sour cream
½ cup ice-cold water
1½ cups all-purpose flour
⅓ cup yellow cornmeal
3 teaspoons sugar, plus 1 tablespoon for sprinkling on the prebaked dough
½ teaspoon salt
10 tablespoons chilled unsalted butter, cut into 8 pieces

FILLING

20 Italian plums, halved and pitted, or 10 of the larger variety plums, quartered
½ cup sugar
2 tablespoons cornstarch
2 teaspoons fresh lemon juice

GLAZE

5 tablespoons plum jam or marmalade
3 tablespoons water
1 tablespoon Grand Marnier or rum

Vanilla ice cream or whipped cream, for serving

* To prepare the pastry, whisk together the sour cream and ice water in a small bowl. Set aside.

* Place the flour, cornmeal, the 3 teaspoons sugar, and salt in a large bowl. Mix with a dry whisk or your fingers until well blended. Add the butter. Mix with your hands, a pastry blender, or in a food processor until the pieces of butter are pea-sized (8 to 10 pulses in the food processor). Add the sour cream mixture, 1 tablespoon at a time, gently mixing after each addition. Once all the liquid has been added, form the dough into a large disk. Don't handle the dough too much, and work quickly so that the butter stays cold. Wrap with plastic wrap and refrigerate for 1 to 2 hours.

* To prepare the filling, while the dough is chilling, place the plums in a large bowl with the sugar, cornstarch, and lemon juice.

* Position a rack in the center of the oven and preheat to 400°F.

* To prepare the glaze, place the jam, water, and Grand Marnier in a small saucepan. Bring to a gentle boil over medium-low heat. Remove from the heat and set aside.

* To prepare the galette, roll out the chilled dough on a lightly floured surface until you have a 14- to 16-inch circle. Lightly flour the top of the dough. Fold the dough over the rolling pin and transfer to an 8-inch cast iron skillet. Gently

press the dough into the bottom and against the sides of the skillet. It just needs to stick to the sides while you add the filling. Arrange the plums in the pan in a circular pattern, slightly overlapping one another, skin side up, starting at the outer edges and working toward the center. Quickly reheat the glaze and spoon over the plums. Fold the edges of the pastry over the fruit. It will form pleats, which is the result you want. You should have a roughly 2- to 3-inch border of dough folded in all around the edges. Sprinkle the plums and crust with the 1 tablespoon sugar. Bake until the crust is golden brown, 25 to 30 minutes. Serve in the skillet with vanilla ice cream or whipped cream.

caramelized apple and gingerbread cake

with Whipped Eggnog Cream

Actually an upside-down cake, this gingerbread is light, fluffy, and incredibly moist. Cooking the apples this way creates a lovely caramel sauce for the top of the cake. The Whipped Eggnog Cream complements the cake.

MAKES 8 TO 10 SERVINGS

CARAMELIZED APPLES

5 tablespoons unsalted butter, cut into 8 pieces
⅔ cup granulated sugar
3 apples (Gala, Fuji, or Golden Delicious), peeled, cored, and cut into 1-inch wedges

GINGERBREAD CAKE

1½ cups water
½ cup molasses
½ cup maple syrup
1 teaspoon baking soda
½ cup (1 stick) unsalted butter, at room temperature
1 cup packed light brown sugar
1 large egg
2½ cups all-purpose flour
½ teaspoon salt
1 tablespoon baking powder
2 teaspoons ground ginger
1 teaspoon ground cinnamon
¼ teaspoon ground or freshly grated nutmeg

WHIPPED EGGNOG CREAM

½ cup heavy cream
½ cup eggnog

* To prepare the apples, melt the butter and sugar in a 10-inch cast iron skillet over medium-low heat. Do not stir. When the mixture begins to caramelize, in 15 to 20 minutes, remove the pan from the heat, and allow it to cool slightly. Arrange the apples in the skillet in a circular pattern, starting from the outer edge and working toward the center. Return the skillet to medium-low heat, and cook the apples for 10 minutes. Remove from the heat and set aside.

* To prepare the cake, bring the water to a boil in a medium saucepan. Remove from the heat and add the molasses, maple syrup, and baking soda. Stir and then set aside to cool.

* Mix the butter and brown sugar in a large bowl, using an electric mixer, until light and fluffy. Add the egg and beat for another 5 to 10 seconds.

* In a separate bowl, sift together the flour, salt, baking powder, ginger, cinnamon, and nutmeg. Using an electric mixer on low speed, add the flour mixture to the butter and brown sugar mixture in thirds, alternating with the molasses mixture. After all the wet and dry ingredients have been added, continue mixing on low speed until all of the lumps are gone and the batter is smooth. Do not overmix.

* Pour the cake batter over the top of the apples in the skillet, being careful not to disturb the apples. Bake until a toothpick comes out clean when inserted in the center of the cake, 30 to 35 minutes. Remove from the oven and let rest for 5 minutes. Run a butter knife around the outside edge of the cake to loosen it. Place a large plate on top of the skillet and, using hot pads, grasp the plate and skillet tightly. Invert the cake onto the plate. Rearrange the apples if any have stuck to the skillet.

* To prepare the eggnog cream, beat the heavy cream and eggnog with an electric mixer until stiff. Serve the cake topped with eggnog cream.

RESOURCES

BOB'S RED MILL NATURAL FOODS
5209 SE International Way
Milwaukie, OR 97222
503-654-3215
www.bobsredmill.com
Grains, cornmeal

TOM DOUGLAS'S RUB WITH LOVE
206-441-4122
www.tomdouglas.com
Spice rubs

LODGE MANUFACTURING COMPANY
P.O. Box 380
South Pittsburg, TN 37380
423-837-7181
www.lodgemfg.com
Our preferred supplier of cast iron cookware

MAMA LIL'S
206-726-8372
www.mamalils.com
Pickled Hungarian goathorn peppers

MORE THAN GOURMET
800-860-9385
www.morethangourmet.com
Demi-glaces, stocks, and other sauces

THE SPANISH TABLE
1427 Western Avenue
Seattle, WA 98101
206-682-2827
www.spanishtable.com
*Spanish olive oils, smoked paprika,
and specialty ingredients*

STAUB USA, INC.
115 Pine Avenue, Suite 640
Long Beach, CA 90802
866-782-8287
www.staubusa.com
*Beautiful and unique cast iron
pieces from France*

SUR LA TABLE
84 Pine Street
Seattle, WA 98101
800-243-0852
www.surlatable.com
*Staub and Le Creuset cast iron pieces
for cooking and serving, splatter guards,
cast iron handle mitts, and a large range
of cookware*

**WASHINGTON STATE
   UNIVERSITY CREAMERY**
101 Food Quality Building
P.O. Box 641122
Pullman, WA 99161-1122
800-457-5442
Cougar Gold cheese

WORLD SPICE MERCHANTS
1509 Western Avenue
Seattle, WA 98101
206-682-7274
www.worldspice.com
Fresh spices and spice blends

INDEX

About the
AUTHORS

SHARON KRAMIS is the author of *Northwest Bounty* (Simon & Schuster) and *Berries: A Country Garden Cookbook* (HarperCollins). A Northwest native, she holds a degree in food science from the University of Washington and is a former food writer for the *Mercer Island Reporter*. Sharon studied with legendary cooking figure James Beard at his summer cooking school in Seaside, Oregon, for six years. She is a founding member of the International Association of Culinary Professionals, Les Dames d'Escoffier's Seattle chapter, and FareStart, a program that trains homeless persons for the hospitality industry. In addition to participating in menu development for Anthony's Restaurants in Seattle, Sharon continues to educate herself through travel and ongoing classes at the California Culinary Academy in Napa Valley. She lives with her husband, Larry, in Seattle.

JULIE KRAMIS HEARNE was brought up with a love for food. When she was young, she would pretend to be sick so that she could stay home from school and watch her mother teach cooking classes, and she often accompanied her mother to James Beard's cooking classes. The former owner of two Seattle restaurants, Julie studied food science and nutrition at Seattle Pacific University, has worked as a restaurant consultant and a food stylist, and spent a year learning at the nationally renowned Herbfarm Restaurant under chef Jerry Traunfeld. Julie is a member of Les Dames d'Escoffier, the International Association of Culinary Professionals, and the Hunger Intervention Program. She continues to learn about food through ongoing classes at the California Culinary Academy in Napa Valley. She lives with her husband, Harker, and three sons in Seattle.

Julie and Sharon have also authored *The Dutch Oven Cookbook* and *Cast Iron Skillet: Big Flavors*. They have traveled all over the country teaching and sharing their passion for cooking in cast iron.